THE BAD DAUGHTER

THE BAD DAUGHTER

by Julie Hilden

1998

ALGONQUIN BOOKS

OF CHAPEL HILL

Published by
ALGONQUIN BOOKS OF CHAPEL HILL
Post Office Box 2225
Chapel Hill, North Carolina 27515-2225

a division of
Workman Publishing
708 Broadway
New York, New York 10003

Published simultaneously in Canada by
    Thomas Allen & Son Limited.
Design by Anne Winslow.

LIBRARY OF CONGRESS CATALOGING-IN-PUBLICATION DATA
Hilden, Julie.
    The bad daughter / by Julie Hilden.
        p. cm.
    ISBN 1-56512-185-6
    1. Hilden, Julie.   2. Mothers and daughters—United States.
3. Alzheimer's disease—Patients—Family relationships.
4. Psychological child abuse—United States.   5. Adult child abuse
victims—United States—Biography.   I. Title.
CT275.H5969A3   1998
306.874'3—DC21   97-32660
                                                  CIP

10 9 8 7 6 5 4 3 2 1
First Edition

For my mother, much too late

In another country people die.

— Anne Sexton

THE BAD DAUGHTER

Prologue

_____

A NORMAL BRAIN'S network of neurons is a beautiful thing: like a graceful willow tree of white electricity coming from the brain stem. Or like a photograph of a firework exploding in a dark sky, its lines of light curving upward and then bending down until, at the ends, they disappear. It is as orderly as the thought it contains. By contrast, a brain with Alzheimer's disease is marked by clotted plaques and tangles of neurons—physical symptoms of dead spots in thought, of lost memory and confusion, disorientation and fear.

In each of the cells in my body, there is a genetic message that determines whether my brain, having been the first type, will inexorably become the second by the time I am fifty or fifty-five. The message is fixed yet inscrutable, immanent yet invisible. It indicates whether my brain will die as my mother's did, in the same process of decay.

As I age, time will burn the message into clarity, as if the friction of its wear had worked the message clear. This would be the more terrible way to learn, the slower. It was the way my mother learned she had the disease, by beginning to die. Or I may be tested and know in a moment what my fate will be. Early-onset Alzheimer's disease, unlike the late-onset kind, is strongly genetically linked. There is a significant chance that I have my mother's gene for the disease, but also a good chance that I have my father's harmless gene instead. It seems so strange to me that I am alive just at the time in history when the test that will tell me whose gene I have is being devised. I will likely know the test's result before the disease comes to me, if it does—and before I decide whether to have children. The doctor who tells me the result will be one of the first empowered to do so—with a power something like fortune-telling, a scrutiny not of the lines on my hand but of its smallest cells. A power coupled with a helplessness, because no one believes the cure will come with the test. It might come much later, so people say.

I have looked for the message in myself. At twenty-nine, I look for any sign of aging. I am waiting to notice a difference, a signal, a line in my skin. If I do have the disease, I wonder whether there will be a moment when it changes into a concrete malignity in me, the thing itself and not its plan or promise. I often wonder: Can I somehow feel in myself, in my body, what the test's result will be? I remember the story that God creates the indentation on the upper lip by laying a finger on it to silence each child in the moment before light, so that the child cannot tell the secrets learned before birth. It is as if my body knows its destiny, and is silent.

For me, this test, which will show whether inherited genes will determine my fate, is the ultimate demonstration of whether the past will always find me, whether it is a real thing that lives inside me, waiting to take me back. In life, I have learned in other ways that even as I try to re-create myself, the past recaptures me. When I was twenty-one, I did not go to my mother when I learned she was dying, and I believed then that I *could* stay away, that I would never be punished for abandoning her. I believed that I could lie casually about what I had done, and the world would never take notice, and that I could live my life separately from hers and not suffer. I found instead that I was punished in many subtle ways for leaving, and that my lying cost me more than I knew. This book is the story of my leaving and what it took from me, and of how I learned I might someday experience the very death I once thought that I could escape, that I had escaped—my mother's.

Chapter One

——

MY MOTHER'S DEATH was a long, blurry process. At the end, there was no memorial service for her, no wake and no tombstone. And no one will ever know exactly when she began dying. But I remember feeling it begin.

I NEVER UNDERSTOOD anything about my parents, not really. As a child, from my room, I couldn't hear what they said when they fought, only the tone and the tenor. Once, when I was very small, I went up to their bedroom door—a balsa wood door resembling a venetian blind—and tried to move the wooden slats so that they would be horizontal and I could look in, or at least hear better, but it was impossible: the wood was fixed still. Eventually, I learned to fall asleep easily and deeply during my parents' fights. Just before sleep, I'd imagine a corner of my room opening to another world, yawning wide while I slept so my spirit could travel through it. This was the escape I would not complete for another ten years.

As I grew older, my mother began to seem to me always tense and irritated—like a fly trapped between window and screen, blocked on all sides, painfully bumping, still flying. She constantly yelled at my father and nothing he did could calm or satisfy her. My parents began to sleep in single beds, with a table set between them. Even at ten I knew what that meant.

When I was small, every April my mother would ring my birthday cake with rabbits constructed from two marshmallows—their eyes and mouths were dots of food coloring; their ears, strips of paper bent around toothpicks. As I got older and my parents' fights became more frequent, she became impatient with the ritual and began instead to use the rows of fused pink marshmallow rabbits that were sold in boxes in the supermarket for Easter. Then, on one birthday—I was nine or ten—the cake she made caved in, swampy at its center. She threw it on the floor dramatically, with a loft; its circular layers separated in the air, disking out in the slippage of icing. After it fell, she leaned against the wall and slid down to the baseboard, crouching, crying, her slippers extending into the mess: the flotsam of exposed toothpicks; rent, spongy cake; and a row of squashed pink rabbits, partially torn from each other, in the midst of it all. I told her that I had not wanted the cake, that she never had to make a cake again. The cake stayed there accusingly for hours, rabbits in a shipwreck of icing. I did not touch it, out of respect for my mother's misery and rage.

My mother was an ambitious woman in ways. At least she talked ambitiously about her life. My father was a professor at the University of Hawaii; she did not work. Before the divorce, she made little motions toward independence: She joined a women's therapy group, bought some Anne Murray records, took some courses at the university toward a master's degree. She decided, for a while, to let her hair go gray; for months, the color line shifted downward until finally the last dyed-blonde ends were cut off. And she left my father.

For a month or so after she left, my mother and I lived in an apartment building in downtown Honolulu with a swimming pool that had a roof deck from which you could see the stars. She would sit there next to me on a deck chair—serene, her hair back, her face serious—and I'd think: Just stay that way and everything will be okay. I made odd, unenforceable bargains with her like that, in my head. I willed her happy. On that deck, it seemed that anything could happen with us; as if an adventure would begin. I was almost ready to embark on it with her.

Yet when she left Hawaii, with me in tow, my mother saw no option but to return to her family—her mother and a set of aunts and uncles with whom she'd grown up—and their New Jersey towns (Chatham, Summit, Madison; we had lived in Kaneohe, Kailua, Manoa). She chose the place she knew, and found a job teaching high school there, just as she had twenty years earlier, before she met and married my father.

She rented a half-house in Chatham for us to live in and filled it with half a marriage's furniture—as if we would share half a life there after the divorce, a continent and an ocean away from my father.

I'd met my mother's family, the Learys, perhaps twice while I was growing up in Hawaii. I knew from the beginning that I did not want to become part of this new, adopted family. They were proper, formal Irish Catholics with a wardrobe of Izod Lacoste and plaid. I still put Sun-In into my hair and wore uneven cutoffs, their threads dangling; T-shirts with fluorescent surf logos; and rubber thongs that chafed between my toes. They had a stocked liquor cabinet and would refill the grown-ups' drinks as soon as they were low. I was averse to drinking, perhaps because I already sensed that my mother drank too much. They were part of an insular community focused on the church and the prep school it ran. A priest from my cousins' school would often come play piano at their house, singing "Danny Boy" in his high range. I went to mass with them once, but I refused communion when it was offered me and I wasn't taken again. I had grown up without religion and did not want it now, though I could tell my mother was ready to return to the Catholicism she had once abandoned.

I felt that my parents' fighting and their divorce had broken me somewhere and I sensed that this new family would not fix this brokenness—maybe they would worsen it. I would be polite, I decided, but the Learys would be my mother's family, not mine. I had my books instead. I was an idealist, an abso-lutist, as a child; I held in my heart the dream of something better. I believed that I could keep myself separate from this family, and from my mother, and then someday leave—pre-serving my damaged state, held together in a mimicry of whole-ness like the composed shards of a broken cup about to be fixed—and never look back. I began to fight with my mother about accompanying her to visit the Learys and eventually she went alone, except on rare occasions.

I think the Learys' house was the only place my mother was truly comfortable after the divorce—with two drinks and a third coming; with references to how, as a child, she had been the messy one whereas her sister, Betty, had been neat. Even when I would not visit the Learys, my mother still told me sto-ries about them, as she had when I was younger and we lived in Hawaii. So, in a way, they remained stories to me even after the move. For her, I think they were the only thing that was real.

My mother loved the sordid flaws of this family as much as she loved its virtues. She told me all the worst stories, in a pru-rient way. How one of my aunts had caught her husband in an affair, finding a lipsticked love note in his pocket. How an-other had come upon a cache of her husband's pornography and he'd said he was no longer attracted to her, but how she'd won him back by spending days walking on the treadmill un-til she lost weight. How my second cousin, who had left graduate school in business because of depression, had tried to kill himself by crashing his head against the toilet bowl, then trying somehow to drown himself in it. My mother held back nothing. In her view, there was no age that was too young to know anything. I think she was very lonely in her life. She wanted me to be with her in it, to be like her. I was thirteen, fourteen when she told me the stories. I wanted to be a child, and not to hear.

LATE ONE NIGHT, a few months after we moved to New Jersey, I came downstairs to find my mother with a man in the kitchen, eating slices of cheesecake from a bakery box. They didn't touch, but I knew they were together from their casualness with each other. I felt the sexuality in it—and I felt the flatness of my chest, my skinniness as I stood there before them. It startled me to see them. I had never seen my mother like that with a man, even my father.

"Can I have some?" I asked, motioning toward the cheesecake, trying to be casual.

"Julie. Of course you can."

Apologetically, my mother rose to greet me, standing taller and heavier than I, as she always would, even as I grew.

"This is John Brunner, a friend of mine from high school," she said.

I remember distinctly the way she looked at that moment. The skin of her face, gray and large-pored in the kitchen's sputtering fluorescent light, her blush red and streaky. Coral lipstick leached into the vertical lines above her upper lip. The flesh beneath her chin was so loose that it almost made a straight diagonal from the tip of her chin to the base of her neck. Her hair, frosted to a white blonde, was cut short and choppily, close to her head. She wore an A-line skirt, a plaid oxford shirt, a pilling gray sweater vest. Her figure was slightly heavy but compact, her breasts a shelf of flesh shored up by a thick-strapped bra. Her stockings were orangy brown; her shoes were like orthopedic shoes, thick-soled and laced up. Her clip-on earrings were whorls of fake gold. I felt sorry for her, but in the way of pity and not of sympathy. I saw her wasted beauty, I saw that it was over for her. And I viscerally feared being her, becoming her.

As a joke, John Brunner stood up, grasped my shoulders, and turned me around so he could look at my ass. He took a long look; he really looked at me.

"Yes," he finally told me. "Go ahead and have some cheesecake."

My mother laughed. She laughed differently when he was around.

I took the plate with the slice back up to my room. As soon as John Brunner had spoken, I'd recognized his deep voice, which caught and rasped. I'd picked up the phone once at our house in Hawaii, just before the divorce, and that was the voice I'd heard.

Perhaps it was for him that she left my father. But this is only speculation. He'd been her high school boyfriend, she told me later. He'd been envied then, the son of the middle-class New Jersey town's most successful car dealer, with his own new Porsche at sixteen. I could tell she still saw him as he had once been: his blond curly hair fine, shiny, and long enough to be rebellious; a rich boy in the town who liked her even though he had his choice of girls.

When my mother returned to him, John Brunner's curls had gone to matted, graying frizz and he wore sunglasses even on shady days. He was gaunt and slightly hunched, with a wispy mustache. His voice was grainy from smoking, his alcoholism so bad that, at one point, my mother joined his family to confront him about it en masse, as a doctor had recommended, lights darkened until he entered the room. He'd almost driven his dead father's car dealership into ruin by inattention, but it was said that his father had hired good salesmen and the business squeaked by.

He was divorced like my mother; his children, a boy named Biff and a girl, lived with his ex-wife, and he lived alone in a country house gone to ruin. Visiting it for the first time, I found it full of Ping-Pong and pool tables set up in rooms that had once been living rooms and children's bedrooms, rooms strewn with toys his children had discarded when they were younger. He lived directly on top of the detritus of his marriage and of his children's early years. He offered me some of the toys, but I was already too old.

He lacked the energy to clean the fishpond on his property, its mouth choked with algae that encroached gradually outward over its surface—in the way it seemed to me that life was engulfing him and my mother, threatening to close over their heads. On one of our visits, he tried to teach me to fish in that decaying pond to impress my mother—talking to her over my head as he helped me bait the hook, his fingers over mine; forcing the worm with difficulty over the fishhook's head, then easily moving it farther down along the thin line of metal.

I might naturally have disliked John Brunner, but I forced myself to like him well enough, and told my mother so. I knew that, whatever his problems, there would at least be safety if my mother married him. I sensed that she needed safety of some sort.

John Brunner and the Learys: my mother's life as it had been twenty-five years ago, now returned to her. It could not quite work—even I sensed it—but she could not resist it. I still think of her, always, as in thrall to her past. It dragged her back to New Jersey from halfway across the Pacific to rejoin her family; it kept her in its hold when she might have started a new life.

It happened that my mother never had a chance to leave the past to which she had returned after the divorce, because she died a death that started early, took a long time, and took everything from her. But I believe she would not have left anyway. If she hadn't become ill, I would have returned, reluctantly, to New Jersey for holidays, to hear the same stories and to watch that family around their long dinner table. She was deeply in love with the past, she was its child, its supplicant. I was falling in love with the future even then, and I equally belonged to it. Maybe that was the simple difference between us; maybe that was why we did not end up loving each other enough, after all.

FOR A LONG time, my mother was always with her family in the evenings or with John. She was very sexual with John when I saw them together—pulling him toward her hips when she hugged him, sitting on his lap—but I knew he did not make her happy. On the nights she saw him, she would still come home and close the door of her bedroom and, no matter how early it was, stay there until morning with the lights out. Sometimes she said she had a headache. Sometimes she did not say anything to explain herself. I would eat dinner alone downstairs, and listen for her moving.

Although I was alone in the house much of the time, I did not feel lonesome. I felt more like a contented bachelor. I spent laborious hours with my homework. It benefited from my entire energy, and I believed it would save my life. And I bided my time by reading. Every other day I borrowed a new book from my history teacher; I don't know if he thought I really read them. After I finished my homework, I would read my borrowed book for four or five hours at a stretch and then fall asleep with the book in the bedclothes, spine cracked, facedown—as if the book were charmed, as if it would protect me. When I went to my room to read, I blocked the rest of the house out of my mind. I did not want to know what was occurring in my mother's room, only a few yards away.

I also had *Masterpiece Theatre*, reruns of the old *Saturday Night Live*. On Sundays, I would take an old silver radio to bed, to fall asleep listening to the Top 40, as if I were a child of a different era. There was a supermarket just past our backyard and I would go buy food at the deli there; I lived mostly on roast beef with salad dressing.

For a while, there was a romance to my life alone, and I could often avoid my mother entirely. She'd conveyed to me implicitly that we were each on our own, and for a while that seemed fine to me. But later my mother took an increasing number of what she called mental health days from her job as a teacher, so that she was there in the house when I returned home after school. I began to worry that she would be fired. She began to drink more, buying jugs of yellow-green Gallo wine from the nearby supermarket every few days. The jugs shone threateningly in the very center of the refrigerator's middle shelf. She saw less of John and spent more time in the house.

Once I interrupted her on a foray to the kitchen, on a day when she had retired to her room as soon as she'd come home. She was sitting at the kitchen table. She stood up and threw the contents of her cup in my face. I flinched and blinked. As the liquid dripped from my face, I tasted it. I expected it to be white wine, but it was clear tea. Maybe she's drinking it to sober up, I thought. I simply wiped it off. She sat down again and looked at the bottom of the cup. I didn't speak to her. I backed out of the kitchen and turned and fled up to my own room. I was too far gone, too detached from this life with her, to cry about it. I was a pragmatist of survival by then and the tea had not hurt me. I could not imagine another mother, another life. I am closer to crying about this moment now than I was then.

As my mother began to spend more and more time at home, I learned that I was no bachelor, but a child, a dependent. By my sophomore year of high school, she would yell and scream at me almost every night when she came home. I had never done anything to provoke her. This is a child's answer, I know: "But I didn't do anything! But it's not my *fault*." It was always the answer I gave; she never believed it; it was always true. Once her checkbook had been stolen and someone was cashing her checks; she thought it must be me. Another time, she thought I was drinking her wine; in truth, I would never have touched it. (For years I would not even drink socially because of her.) I think she blamed me for the wine because she literally could not believe how much she had drunk the previous night, because she mistook her own capabilities, still had a sense of herself that was better than what she had become.

As she became more and more displeased with me, my mother began to fight with my father loudly on the phone about who would pay my expenses; she cataloged for him each dollar she spent on me so that I could hear. And she would often threaten me: "If you don't like it here, you can always go live with your father."

I was afraid I would have to test this threat sometime, only to find out that I could not go. My father had gotten remarried to a woman who had her own daughter, Kara, a child model. He had sent me a picture of the wedding, with Kara as the flower girl, wearing a lei. They all lived together in a condo in Hawaii. When I saw the photo, how they were a family in it, I began to know that the life with my mother was the only one I would be permitted to have.

My father would call to check on me, but he had never invited me to live with him. When he called, it became increasingly awkward to talk to him—as if each month I knew him less. As if a hundred awkward conversations, and the passing of time, would eventually make us wholly strangers. I don't know if he knew how bad it was with my mother; he must have had a sense. I loved him, but I was not sure if he would take me back. And I knew it would be a crushing blow to my mother if I ever accepted her offer and actually left. I knew I would go, if I went, only when she wanted me to. Her telling me I could leave was a taunt, a way to keep me scared and obedient, to confirm for me that I was trapped or to make me grateful to her. I had the feeling that she was keeping me with her out of shame—because as a mother she was supposed to, she *must*, she must *want* to—that I would shame her irremediably if I ever asked to leave.

I missed my father and took irrational comfort in the fact that it was he, not my mother, I resembled—the strict T our noses and brows made was the same—as if that meant that his calmness, his stability and sanity, were also my inheritance. My mother could not claim a single feature that we shared. Even the Learys could not stretch a point to claim a resemblance. It simply was not there.

Even living so far from my father, I told myself I was still essentially his child: charmed like him, protected like him. If I could not be with him, it was enough that I was *like* him. Though in many ways my father was lost to me, I believed at some level that he and I were the lucky ones of the family— excelling in school, hyper-rational, careful to exercise, rarely sick. Blessed, we'd be protected, and danger would pass, as if tall angels bent over us until we were encircled, making a tent with their huge wings, the end-feathers brushing the ground.

My mother, I thought, was the one who would always be out of control, unprotected in the middle of the world, wronged in her own eyes and raging, always in grief. She was the one who was so often ill, with her migraines, the one who drank. Everything would be borne by her, I thought. My father and I would be exempted from her destiny.

Eventually, my mother's anger at the world became a presence in the house so palpable it gave me stomach pains. The muscles in my abdomen clenched tight at the mere sound of irritation in her voice. I came to know her anger intimately, judged its ebbs and flows, judged what I could ask for and what was impermissible. She gave me a set of chores; I did them all. She set a curfew; I followed it. I learned never to act without thinking, and above all never to argue back. I felt like a trapped thing: crafty, calculating how to live under the caprice of her anger.

I never invited friends to the house, because of my mother's screaming. Indeed, it is not too much to say that I did not really *have* friends in high school, because if I did then someday they would want to come to the house. Chatham was a middle-class commuter town where the parents worked in New York City, or in New Jersey banks and corporations. It was all white, all Christian, with very few divorces. The high school had state championship teams in soccer and football. It believed fervently in proms and pep rallies and cheerleaders. All the girls in the senior class were automatically on the ballot for homecoming court, whether they wanted to be or not. It was assumed you would want to be among the elect; it was a town where *they* chose *you*. Or did not. I felt that I could not risk the town's knowing about us. It was more than a feeling of shame, it was a feeling that it was somehow subversive for my mother and me to live there, that we might not be allowed to live there anymore if people knew.

MY MOTHER LOVED murder mysteries and true crime, especially Truman Capote's *In Cold Blood*. On her days off, she stayed in bed to read them. And she liked learning about crime nearby. Driving at night with me on a winding back road near the Learys', she told me how a girl had recently been killed there, how the girl, driving, was bumped from the back, stopped, and was knifed. And when my mother took the wrong exit and ended up lost with me in the depressed inner city of Paterson, she told me that we weren't safe in the car, because black kids would gather around cars and rock them, to force the occupants out. She once showed me a tabloid headline—MOM KILLS KIDS AND SELF—and I knew for certain she would never do it, yet I knew also that the thought of ending this life with me, here, was not unpleasant to her. Instead, in her mind, it was funny and kitschy and almost possible. She liked to scare me, in the hope that I would appreciate her more.

I did not fear her exactly, but I feared the days with her, feared enduring them, feared how many they would be.

The summers were the worst. As a high school teacher, my mother had the summers off. This meant there was no money in the summer. And there was nowhere to go but the town, in which I had no friends. My mother would not allow me to learn to drive—she was afraid of teaching me and would not pay for lessons. This was odd, because she herself loved driving, loved big American boats of cars that were like a living room you rested in, loved manipulating her blue Chevy as it took its wide turns. She tried to teach me once and kept gripping the handle of the passenger door as if she would throw herself out of the car and leave the crash I was sure to cause. It was a small town with quiet streets and a low speed limit; there was no danger. Yet I did not learn to drive; I learned her fear of it instead. It still is with me.

And I learned to sleep twelve hours a day for those summer months, like an animal waiting for its Spring. When I awoke, it was midday; it was already hot.

Once my mother's childhood friend Elayne visited us in the summer. Elayne was a high school principal and counselor, perceptive about teenagers, and she asked me, "What do you *do?*" I think she could tell that there were days when I did nothing, spoke to no one, read books in the house that I had read many times before, in a cursory way, so that I could appear to be reading.

I muttered something about hanging around, about movies; mentioned the names of girls in my classes—Amy, Heather, Eleni—and said they were my friends. I could see my mother was proud of me for lying. I knew that she would leave me alone for a few days because I had vouched for her in front of Elayne, for our being normal.

LIVING MY SEPARATE life next to my mother, I began to lose the sense that I loved her, or that I ever had. I could remember that I had loved her, but not the feeling of it. When I was a child, she had been able to break my heart in a second— once, by not wearing a plastic sea horse necklace I'd given her; once, by not noticing my report card on the table. I had excelled in school to please her. I had learned to read before I'd gone to school to please her—because of the excitement in her face when she knew that I could. I had wanted that excitement—more than the words, more than the meaning that reading brought. My life was a show for her when I was a child. Now I excelled at school not out of joy but out of fear, and any gift I gave her was to allay her anger.

Love does end; it *is* extinguished. At least, this was what I learned from my mother. The divorce, she felt, had erased more than fifteen years of marriage. Thirteen of those erased years had been my life. My parents had moved to Hawaii together when I was one; all I'd known was that place, and their marriage. After the divorce, my mother would not speak of those thirteen years with my father and me. She spoke instead only of the present, and of her childhood and youth with her family. I never heard my parents' courtship story; I came of age to hear it just as my mother began to deny that it had meant anything, when she began, implicitly, almost to deny it had occurred. And my mother was not like other parents, who will tell their children—to their apparent embarrassment and secret pleasure—what they were like when they were young. I never learned from my mother about the child I had been. I sensed that, to her, my childhood was inessential or moot, part of a long mistaken trip she had taken before returning home.

In my tatami slippers, with their felt thongs and bamboo soles, and my surfer shirts, I must have been a living memory of Hawaii, and of my father, for her—the continuity between two lives that thwarted the perfect escape she wanted. Did she see my father in me, in the way I was calm and rational, the way I did not raise my voice and left her to rail and scream, to feel that she inflicted herself upon me? Like him, I suffered her rages, and did not rise to meet them—as if I knew that was what would hurt her most. She needed rage to meet rage—it had, in her own family. She and her father had screamed at each other nightly, but I knew that she'd cried bitterly, inconsolably when he died. My mother needed to tangle, and subside; maybe that was love, to her. The intimacy of fighting, of hot anger. We never gave her that, my father and I. Like him, I would never come to her, and I never really understood her. And, like him, I was punished for my failure to know her, and the punishment was that she left me—and if she did not put a continent and an ocean between us, there was enough space in the hallway between our bedrooms to create the same effect.

The time just after the divorce may have been the very beginning of her dying—but we did not know. The divorce was an easy scapegoat: it could be invoked to explain everything, to excuse, to overshadow. Yet I sensed dimly that my mother's anger, which had sometimes flared in my parents' fights before the divorce, had gradually begun losing focus even as it became more frequent. It spun out, diffuse, a messy anger that often had no actual object, or if it had an object, it was one manufactured out of paranoia—my drinking her wine, another teacher in the school who she said was out to get her. It was as if something were hurting her, making her lash out with more force but less direction than before—as if at an unseen assailant, an invisible destroyer. Sometimes when she screamed at me it sounded like keening, as if she were in grief over her own anger.

The first doctor my mother saw gave her a prescription for painkillers, sent her to a psychiatrist to talk about her divorce, and told her she must be having particularly bad migraines brought on by stress. She did not wholly believe the doctor even then, sensing that her headaches signified something more than tension, that her blurry vision was something more than glasses could ever correct.

Once, just after parking the Chevy in a supermarket lot, she folded her arms on the steering wheel, laid her bowed head on them, and said in a whisper, "I don't know what's happening to me."

Hearing her whisper, I thought only that the breakdown I'd expected for so long, ever since the divorce, had finally come. Day by day, I waited for it, waited for her breaking. I wondered how people went crazy. Would it just be the same thing but more? Would it be a different thing altogether? I did not have a lock on my bedroom door to lock against her; I locked my mind and heart against her instead.

I STARTED TO have dreams in which a presence, restless and aware, stalked us, padding through the rooms of the half-house. It took different forms. Sometimes it was unthinkably huge, its face as big as the night sky, staring out at me through the cataract of drifting clouds. Sometimes it was small and domestic and insinuating, like a cat. At times it was even smaller, small enough to flatten itself and slip through the space under doors. In dreams, I kept very still for fear of it, shutting my eyes tightly to avoid watching its face. Twin cones of light, starting at its eyes and widening outward into round spot-lights, touched me with their orbs of cold but never rested. They rested elsewhere, in another room.

I GRADUATED FROM high school in three years, on the pretext that the high school did not have enough advanced courses, but really to escape her. I wonder if anyone at the school saw through my explanations or, rather, how completely they did. And if my mother did, too. I think she would walk into my room, see me with my head bent over my books, and know that her intense, serious daughter was striving with all her will and energy simply to be able to leave her and never to look back. A survival instinct kept me creepily focused. When I read, I had a preternatural concentration so that I could not hear my mother's voice even if, several times, she might speak my name. She would have to raise her voice to reach me.

I was driven and frozen at the same time, waiting to grow up only so I could get away, lonely without realizing it. I could not live now the way I lived then, my life reduced to its skeleton. Then I was focused only on surviving, leaving, obsessed by these things. If I could have gone to sleep one night at any time during high school and awakened seventeen years old and on my way to college, I would have chosen that. I would have given over four years of life in a moment.

When I received Harvard's letter of acceptance, the feeling I had was primarily not joy but relief: it was the ticket out. The relief disappeared when the financial aid letter came. My mother said she would not pay her thousand-dollar contribution. I did not understand then that there were government and private loans to which I could resort, that the school would make it possible for me to go, somehow. I thought it all depended on her whim, as so much of my life had for the past four years. For weeks, I felt the world darken around me, as if it were about to close up. Finally my father said he would pay her thousand-dollar share as well as his own. I could go.

Thus, as my mother was beginning the long process of her dying, I began the process of my leaving—as I had left in my heart long ago. I did not hate her, but the love I had for her as a child was gone; it seemed distant, confined to an earlier time. And I believed that I needed to leave her to survive her —as if whatever was happening to her, the breakdown, the dissolution, were contagious; as if I would wake up one day in her room or even in her mind, and leave my own forever. And I believed in divorce, I had learned from it. I believed that she had left me first, and with a child's logic I thought that made leaving her right.

I believed then that you could jettison your family, as if it were the part of a rocket that falls away, and falls apart, even as the rocket is speeding forward. Does it need to be said, I wonder, that in leaving I fell apart, inside, instead—soundlessly and unbeknownst to myself? I did not know that I had, though, for a long time, and for the moment, as I graduated from high school, I felt free, as if the world were open to my heart's plans.

Chapter Two

———

THE DAY I arrived at Harvard, I had my acceptance letter safe with me in my pocket—as if the college might change its mind and challenge my admission there. I felt an odd, official sense of my entitlement to buy and wear a college sweatshirt. My first night there, I paced back and forth in my small dorm room with its bare, blue-striped mattress, in a building right on Harvard Yard, unable to sleep, waiting for something to happen, convinced that it would.

I knew I could make myself up there at college, perhaps from books, creating a persona that could be punctured, that was built on paper, but that could also be animated and become real. It struck me that night—and then more deeply the first time I stayed out until four in the morning without consequences, without my mother having to know—that the wall, or perhaps the bridge, of books I'd been building was complete. I believed that I'd successfully left my mother in order to live in books, in the space they created.

I chose to major in philosophy, partly because the department was small. I learned about logic, and about how one should ideally live. All the moral hypotheticals were about marooned parties of travelers deciding which of their members should be cannibalized, or whether one should reroute a runaway train so that it would kill a smaller, different set of people on another track. All the questions were about utilitarianism versus Kantianism versus the theory of John Rawls. The result was that I studied ethics—moral reasoning, Harvard called it—and received the highest grade in a class in it, without once thinking about my mother.

At college, I acquired a group of friends that made itself into a patched-together simulacrum of family: that is, of our dream of it, not of the families we actually had. Dining-hall dinners with my friends, their repartee comforting and intimate, were what I imagined meals in intact families must be like. I tried to be cool and not to betray to them that they were the first friends I had really had.

You could be just like anyone else there at college, I found. There were sixteen hundred people in a class, most of them trying not to be the people they had been in high school, all in different ways. It was a school for deception—romantic deception, perhaps, to put it more charitably. I began slowly to feel at home walking up the broad steps of Widener Library, between its stately pillars, lying with a book in the lush green of the Yard, or curling into the hollows of the golden Henry Moore sculpture there. I began gradually to feel that I belonged in this beautiful place.

WHEN I CAME home to New Jersey my first summer, I found my mother's new apartment in chaos. In the bedroom, the floor was littered with tampons and white half-slips, pools of silk. In the living room, M&M's, spilling out of a bag, were crushed into the ridges of the carpet, their colored shells cracked, the chocolate spread to paste. Ants were gutting them, creating a colorful trail away from the candy bag into the walls.

I opened one of the narrow kitchen cabinets to find it filled ceiling-high with a precarious tower of tubby jugs of Gallo wine. I shut the cabinet door immediately but not abruptly, careful in case the bottles might fall. At first I felt I could choose not to know this about my mother, this certain confirmation that she was now an alcoholic like John Brunner. If I had seen it for only a moment, I could simply forget. But later the sight of the bottles in their sculptural balance would come to me like a snapshot at random times.

No bed was available for me to use, so I made up a mattress on the floor. Walking around Chatham, living there with my mother, I saw that the half-house in which we had lived had been converted into office space, and my high school to a middle school—as if the town had collaborated with me in the erasure of my past. I applied for jobs at all the stores and businesses in the town, without success. My mother refused to give me a ride so that I could temp farther away, at the huge AT&T complex nearby, but she still screamed at me for not being able to get a job. I think she was afraid for me, afraid that I wouldn't be able to manage the contribution Harvard said I had to make to my tuition. I don't know why she felt she couldn't help me.

I left her, to live in Philadelphia near my boyfriend and to temp. She curled up in her bed and cried as I was leaving. I had not even believed my leaving would move her. I had believed she wanted me gone. It mattered to me that she could cry for me this once—out of her fear for me and over losing me for the summer. For years, I knew, she had cried bitterly by herself, for herself, cried for all the causes of her sorrow and anger—and she had included me among them. Yet her crying did not change my mind. I had been hurt so deeply by her, left so alone for so long, that the feeling did not admit of counter-examples or revisions. I had felt this way for so long that I identified the feeling with my deepest self. And ultimately I did not feel any compunction to stay. On the contrary, I felt elated because I no longer had to, she could not tell me to, because I did not have to dully assent and be obedient and quiet and confined to my room.

My boyfriend and his friend picked me up and we drove to

Philadelphia with the radio on loud. I felt a new sense of freedom in the world, of being young and in a car and free, as
others had been during the high school years I had endured
instead of living.

AT FIRST, NO one at school knew very much about my mother.
I ached for someone to know me well enough to guess. I knew
it was unreasonable to want people to read my mind, but often I did want that. Asking for sympathy would ruin things, it
seemed, and I was too proud, anyway, to ask.

I met the woman who would become my best friend in college, Sarah, during my sophomore year. She was thin to a
point just short of anorexia. The day I met her, nothing she
was wearing matched—not the olive green military-surplus
sweater with the multicolored flag patch at the shoulder or the
faded blue-white narrow jeans or the burgundy loafers. But
Sarah herself matched. Her nearly black eyes matched her
dark hair, and her eyes' clear whites, like stones polished by a
river, matched her dead-white skin. Her earrings, composed
of multiple nested silver triangles, and her oversized, silver-
framed reading glasses made a metal junkyard, a sort of des-
olate site, of her lovely face.

Like me, Sarah was reclusive and bookish, frightened and
spooky and easily spooked. Something in her eyes bespoke
early sorrow and later safety, some wariness mixed with relief.
We had both been kept in our mothers' eyries for too long, so
that we were not entirely fitted to live in the world when we

finally emerged. And by the time we came to college, both of us lived essentially without a mother. Mine was angry, depressed, and ill; Sarah's, unstable, a wraith—a tiny-boned, tentative woman who hid in the family's Brooklyn Heights apartment, shrinking into a silk dressing gown, her lemur eyes large-socketed, wearing burgundy lipstick too dark for her pale face. (I met her once; my own mother had long ago become too shameful, I thought, for any friend to meet.)

Sarah and I toiled compulsively over our schoolwork. Sarah had been at the top of the class freshman year, had won a prize for it. She double-majored in biology and English and took a double load each semester. I was almost equally compulsive. Both of us thought that, without a toehold at school, we would fall back into the abyss of our families. Control, or the semblance of control, was priceless to us. We would have given anything to be assured that we would not be like our mothers, and we were driven in all things by the fear that we would be.

It was, of course, to Sarah that I first spoke of my mother, and my friendship with her was the first experience in my life since childhood that felt anything like a love.

BY THE END of my time in college, when I spoke to my mother on the phone from school in the evenings, she would segue in and out of coherence. I talked *at* her for minutes on end—chattering on about my classes just so as not to hear her painful, halting voice. She spoke whole sentences that were perfectly clear, but sometimes stray words from prior or later sentences would find their way in. She would pause for a long time, unable to recall an everyday word. Finally I'd supply it and she'd repeat it several times, as if she could take it back that way and hold it in her mind.

Once I asked her if there was anything I could do for her, and she told me, "You just be Julie." I still don't know what she meant—if it was generous of her not to ask anything of me or if this was a reproach against my solitariness. You would have to have known the tone of her voice to interpret what she said, and the tone of her voice, when she spoke to me those evenings, was no longer a stable thing.

Sometimes it seemed that, picking up the phone and hearing my voice, she pulled herself back from another, faraway place. But once I called her late in the evening and she answered in gibberish that never sorted itself out. Frightened, I hung up. When I called the next day, neither of us mentioned it.

In retrospect, I think she was drinking heavily in the evenings, when I usually called. At that time, she still had not lost her job as a teacher—she would not for several more years—so she must have managed to remain articulate enough in the daytime. I think it was the combination of the alcohol and the beginning of the Alzheimer's disease that undid her in the nighttime; that scrambled and slurred her words until they could not be understood, as if they were spoken over a gathering wind.

Chapter Three

————

I CHOSE TO attend law school in part because of my mother.
Sometimes her life seemed to catch only at the edges of mine
as I drew away from qualities that were hers: hysteria, weak-
ness, and especially the expression of anger. But sometimes
the drive to avoid repeating her life became much more specific. I did not major in English in college precisely because
she had. I went to law school to become the professional
woman her family would never have encouraged her to be.

I had begun to discard the objects that reminded me of my
mother: not all at once, as a statement, but gradually over time,
as I came upon them in a succession of moves during the summers. A few cards she'd sent to me at college. Photographs
from the time I'd lived with her. Even the high school yearbook picture for which she'd chosen my dress, even though—
or maybe because—buying the broad-collared, pretty dress
had been, for once, a nice thing she'd done for me: more than

she could afford. The picture was of me, but I thought she was there in it, in the choice of the dress, and that alone made the picture unacceptable, made me rip it up and made me throw away the yearbook.

I learned, of course, that memory doesn't end—even if you get rid of all the things that are supposed to prompt it. The photos I'd thrown out, and the words on the cards, yielded to images, fragmented phrases, to a sort of unlocalized memory of pain. The memories never disappeared entirely. They were just kept in my mind in shards. I could not forget my mother, though I tried. I was haunted by the thought of return, of returning to her, of having a different life with her than the one we had had. I could not forget her for a day.

Still, even if I could not wholly rid myself of memories by ridding myself of cards and photos, I nevertheless liked thinking of my life as stripped down, silent on the topic of my mother. A life without evidence of sorrow.

When I arrived at Yale, I chose to live in the law school's single building, which held classrooms, dormitory, and library all together, connected by corridors and underground tunnels. Its architecture is faux Gothic: the long, ornate main corridor is legendarily compared to a Gothic bowling alley. Over its gateways, maxims from famous lawyers and judges are cut in stone. The library's vaulted ceiling is covered with reliefs of medieval beasts, griffins and basilisks. I haunted that library and its leather chairs at all hours, driven by the overwhelming importance of my grades—which would determine, with a frightening predictability and finality, whether I'd make law journal, and whether a good judge or firm would hire me when I graduated.

I was teased by friends because the questions I asked in class were never really questions, but interpretations that I offered, waiting to see if they would be accepted by the professor. There were implicit questions beneath my "questions," though: "Am I right? Will I be a good lawyer? Is there a place for me here?" And even: "Will this place save me?" I needed it to.

Before each of my exams, I stayed up all night in the library, and then, in the early morning, sat on a picnic table in the courtyard—licking the pink icing off a doughnut, watching the dawn, and forcing myself through exhaustion to continue to read. I could not differentiate the drive that comes from intellectual interest from the drive that comes from fear. I thought the law could provide the strand of linear reasoning that would lead me out of my past, my family—hand over hand, conclusion by conclusion—like the trail of string that solved the Minotaur's maze.

The law school had exams after Christmas, a practice that drew criticism from the students each year, yet was never changed. This practice both advantaged me over other students and gave me something to do over the winter breaks. I always remained at school to study, almost alone in the Gothic building. Around my windows I would put up white Christmas lights, which lit up the icicles outside so that they cast clear shadows on the window frame. Typing on my computer keyboard, I would bring my space heater—its red bar glowing behind a protective grille—so close to my legs that it slowly singed the hairs off my calves as I worked. The radiator in my dorm room banged and coughed.

Over those breaks, I lost myself in areas of legal doctrine, as if they were places I could be—following hypothetical companies through bankruptcy reorganizations and out again into liquidity; envisioning possible corporate takeovers, the auctions with their tense bidding; diagramming the flow of made-up streams of money to decide when income was "realized" so that it should be taxed. Those legal worlds were so compelling to me. They were consummately rational. And they bore the promise that, if I studied hard enough, I could understand them, that my understanding would inexorably deepen with work.

The law school in winter always seemed to have a light coating of snow that mounded on the building's various gargoyles with their craggy faces. But through my windows, the snowflakes swirling down outside seemed unreal, like artificial snow in a shaken paperweight. I did not really experience those winters; I was elsewhere.

The grades I wanted eventually came, but with such difficulty, with constant and compulsive work. For my boyfriend Aaron they came so easily. As a law student, I was a theorist at heart, interested in hypotheticals and prone to digressions.

Aaron was different. He finished his schoolwork with merciless efficiency and only the exact amount of time and thought required. He was my precise opposite as a lawyer: a "letter of the law" man who paid little attention to its spirit and was scornful of the theory behind it. A consummate pragmatist and a believer in realpolitik, he chose as his idols New York's successful corporate lawyers, not the law professors who taught us. For Aaron, the law was a way to advance in the world, to acquire control over it. For me, it was an alternate world into which I could escape, separate from the real one.

AS I WAS learning a language—the law's strange idiom—my mother was increasingly losing one. As I gained a way to understand the world, it was, at the same time, slipping further and further from her grasp.

At about the time I started law school, doctors first listed alternative diagnoses for my mother's illness. When she told me the diagnoses, I felt that I was learning the possible names of that animal presence of my dreams, learning to name what I had for a long time somehow known.

For several years, CAT scans and MRIs had shown nothing, and my mother had managed to function in her job as a teacher despite her symptoms: the headaches, occasional disorientation, difficulty in seeing that glasses could only partially correct. The New Jersey doctors who had been puzzled before now said that despite the negative brain scans, my mother's increasing symptoms could indicate Creutzfeldt-Jakob syndrome, a type of brain virus. Or maybe an incipient brain tumor, too small yet to show. Or (but this was more rare) early-onset Alzheimer's disease, the same disease old people get but with an early occurrence—in the victim's fifties or sixties, sometimes even in the late forties. My mother was forty-eight then. This last was the diagnosis that turned out later to be true.

Only a few months after her own mother—my grandmother Nan—died, my mother was finally forced to leave her job as a high school teacher because of her illness, with only a small disability pension. The trouble had started when students began to be puzzled by her written comments on their papers. She'd begun to repeat and ramble in class, too. Finally, the school board asked her to resign.

My Aunt Betty told me later that my mother had stayed in the classroom longer than she should have, keeping up a pretense with her colleagues by simply avoiding contact with them as much as she could. For a while, the children she taught were afraid to tell their parents about her, fearful of disrupting routine. At first some had thought they were the only ones who didn't "get" her comments. Then they'd started talking among themselves. Perhaps they looked at each other nervously in class, wondering who would be the first to "tell" on the teacher, to go to the principal—the smart kids, worried about their education, or the backward kids, wanting to get the teacher in trouble for once.

After she lost her job, my mother moved into my grand-mother's apartment, which she'd inherited. At some point John Brunner left her, I don't know when. When she told me he'd left, I imagined him alone in his many-roomed house, aimlessly hitting Ping-Pong balls into a space with no one to return them. I imagined the coating of algae reaching the edge of his pond, and the fish dying there under its thick green car-pet before they could be fished up by him to flip and fight and die on land. I realized I still had a small silver bear on a chain that he'd given me, on a birthday when it seemed that he and my mother might marry. I'd never worn it.

It was creepy for me to think of my mother living amidst the furniture my grandmother had moved to New Jersey from her Cape Cod house. The couches slipcovered in navy-blue-and-white plaid. The wooden rocking chair with a ship's tiller carved into its back. The lamps encircled with painted sea-gulls, their wings brush strokes of lacquer. Dishes of seashells on every end table, and glass fishermen's globes hanging from the ceiling in nets of hairy twine. The painted wooden fisher-men, six inches high, with their black pipes and yellow slick-ers. And the seagulls on wires so that, if you squinted, you could think they flew.

My mother told me on the phone that she'd started baking my grandmother's trademark sour cream coffee cakes. I envi-sioned the flour-speckled recipe still posted on the refrigerator, written in my dead grandmother's distinctive, scratchy hand;

thought of the bubbles bursting on the coffee cakes' surfaces in the oven, falling back into warm craters lined with cinnamon and sugar.

But my mother couldn't cook my grandmother's recipes for long. Her eyesight steadily worsened and eventually, she told me, she had to give up cooking. Living on canned and packaged food, with nothing to do, she slid into obesity in a matter of months. She became much as my grandmother had been: weak, heavy, lethargic. It seemed she never left the house; sometimes one of the Learys would visit her, bringing food or other necessities. On the phone, I heard her heavy breathing at any physical effort: to reach across the telephone table, to rise from her chair. She was just fifty. She was already old.

She had great difficulty making out small numbers and letters. My aunt Betty, who lived in Tucson, sent her a telephone with huge square buttons pre-programmed with all her relatives' numbers; a tape recorder with a set of Steven Wright comedy tapes, whose dry humor my mother listened to over and over, until she would quote it to me on the phone; and a clock that announced the time in a sterile voice, on the hour and whenever she depressed its triangular top. In the background of my phone calls with my mother I could hear the digitized voice of that clock intone eerily on the hour. My mother had no appointments and few visitors, but she frequently, anxiously consulted the clock, invoking that neutered voice—"The time is now . . ."—to break up the time, to make it thinkable and bearable, to follow the old routine of day and night and time: time for breakfast, lunch, and dinner; time to listen to the talk show hosts she heard but couldn't fully see.

She was declining; I was frozen. I had no money and I could not bring myself to leave school. But it was clear that something had to change, to break or to give.

It was my aunt who stepped into this situation.

I don't know exactly what horror happened with my mother in New Jersey in the months before Aunt Betty arrived, while I was safely cosseted at Yale, but my aunt told me a little of it.

"Julie. Your mother is with me now," Betty announced over the phone. "I've been too busy moving her stuff to call you. The last few days have been a nightmare. Thank God she's out of New Jersey. She was almost blind when I came to get her, but she knew her way to the liquor store all right," she said, and laughed her hard laugh, so like my mother's that it sounded to me for a moment as if my mother were laughing at her own fate.

I thought of the cashiers watching my sad mother come in day after day, trying to read the liquor labels and to tell apart the faces on the bills she held.

"She had to be moved," my aunt said. "She took a shower and couldn't turn it off. The tub ran over, and she was totally helpless, Julie, jumping up and down. The neighbor knocked because the ceiling leak was filling the pans on his stove. He turned the shower off and then he called the police. He thought she was crazy. I don't blame him. The police got me on the automatic dial, and I flew right in.

"I told her it would be a visit," my aunt continued, "but there's no way she's going back there. She's staying with me now, then she goes to a home."

My aunt paused. "Now she takes baths. She only runs a trickle so it takes an hour to fill. It's driving my kids crazy. They can never get in to pee."

"It's more than blindness," Betty continued. "She forgot where the tap should be, Julie. She forgot there was such a thing as a tap.

"It's time for you to do your part," she added. "Why don't you come out to Tucson and help me move her into the home, and we can figure out a place for you to work out here for a while. Later we can trade off taking care of your mother. I'll do it for a few years, then you can do it for a few years."

I didn't say anything. I was partially in shock. I had not known that things with my mother were so bad—or I had known and not known at the same time. I had known but not been able to bear it, or to act.

"You come out here, Julie," my aunt said loudly. "You come out here right now."

I hung up on her, out of panic.

This can't happen, I thought. Not now, not after years of school, not when my real life is about to begin. Not when I had fled so far and, it had seemed, so successfully.

I knew that I had to call Betty back, that I couldn't ever hang up on her again. From now on, she might be my only connection with my mother. If she got too angry at me, I might lose touch with my mother entirely. I would have no way to reach her, or hear about her, at all.

Like the rest of the Learys, Betty had been a virtual stranger to me when I was growing up. My strongest memory of her was of a time she'd called the Learys' during Thanksgiving dinner and asked to speak with each member of the family. When she tried to talk to me, I shifted the cordless phone to my other hand and passed her voice, still talking, over the mashed potatoes and on to another of my mother's relatives. I knew that I did not want this family's intimacies, then or ever. But now I had no choice.

So I called Betty and apologized and thanked her for what she'd done, and in turn Betty began to write and call me frequently, to update me on what was going on with my mother. She told me she came to check on my mother at her nursing home frequently; Betty was my mother's only outside contact for long periods. She celebrated my mother's birthday with her, alone. She made sure my mother had the medical care she needed.

She was the hero of my mother's life.

And she became a nightmare to me, persistent and demanding. There was no middle ground for her. I had to move to Tucson and leave school. Later, I had to accept my several-year rotation as the primary person to care for my mother.

"Your mother took care of you," she said. "Now it's time for you to take care of her."

I think Betty sensed the ambivalence in me and believed that there must be, at a deep level, love for my mother there —and that she could reach it if she described my mother's plight plaintively and frequently enough. She was right that love for my mother was there in me, I think, wrong only in believing it could ever be reached. At nine, I had still loved her. By the time I was fourteen, that love was mostly inaccessible to me. By the time I was twenty-one and faced with the question of whether to help her, if any love remained in me, it was like the unseen center of a Russian doll—below many layers of flight and fear, and willful forgetting.

I vacillated for a while, never saying yes, and finally I told Betty no. She became mean then. She taunted me, crowing, because I had Alzheimer's disease on both sides. (My father's mother—my stately, elegant grandmother, Rita, whom I loved in a miraculous, easy way, without question—had begun to get it too.) She told me that I'd get mine, one way or the other. My just deserts would come to me, she said. She told me I was a bad person, that she could tell this from when I was little.

I began to hate my mother then, and that hatred was convenient. It meant I could focus on her cruelty and not on my own failures. For a while, I managed to miss the point that the question of whether I would visit my mother, whether I would help her, was not just an argument between me and my aunt. It was a question I needed to put to myself, seriously.

SOON AFTER BETTY brought my mother to Tucson and started calling me frequently, I visited Sarah at the private school in Connecticut where she taught biology and French. She was unhappy there. The faculty men, she said, made passes at her behind their wives' backs, intrigued by her Russian features, so different from those of the tan, athletic blondes they'd married. The students, she complained, were shallow, with a false sophistication that made them chatter on in mimicry of their parents, blithely discussing adults' affairs and business deals with an affected familiarity.

In Sarah's suite of rooms, waiting for her to return from teaching, I noticed an open school notebook on the bed, its cover bearing no title, only the familiar grade-school mottle of black and white. The exposed page held a family tree sketched in pencil. Sarah's mother's side of the page was carefully pencil-darkened with neat crosshatches; her father's side, untouched. The circle representing Sarah was placed on her mother's side behind the pencil slashes. Her sister's circle was on her father's side, suspended in its clear field.

I put the notebook aside, realizing Sarah shared my secret fear that I would inherit my mother's fate somehow, as a birthright, that the darkness that had shadowed my mother would be cast over my life as well. I didn't speak to Sarah about the notebook, but I did tell her about my mother.

"Don't go back," Sarah said confidently. "My father made the same decision. His mother was sick, his relatives begged him to stay. He still went to college. He doesn't regret it."

"I might regret it," I said.

"You'll regret staying back with her," Sarah said. "Not doing what you wanted. You'll regret what you lost, what you could have done."

What Sarah said gave me the courage to be afraid—not afraid of my mother, but afraid for myself. I had always associated leaving her with survival itself. Now I felt that I could not even visit, that I had to stay away in order to live. The fear that had been born in my years with my mother had not changed. I feared that merely by visiting I would move into my aunt's demesne and that she would have expansive power over me, just as my mother had. My aunt was so like my mother: the sound of her loud voice, her insistence, the way she berated me. To visit my mother while she was in my aunt's care felt like retracing an escape. I feared—it was crazy, I know—that if I visited, my aunt would somehow keep me there, in the world from which I had fled long ago. And if she kept me I would never escape, because I did not have the strength to escape twice.

Irrational as my fear was, it was so strong that it did no good to try to argue myself out of it—as if to say to someone,

"That is only a spider," or an elevator, or an airplane, when to that person it is the embodiment of every childhood fear.

I feared returning not just to my mother's world but also to her time. For my mother, time had looped backward, over and over, when she'd returned to the towns of her youth, to the Learys and John Brunner, and later when she'd taken over my dead grandmother's apartment and her life—until my aunt had to transport my mother to Tucson, where it was as if time had stopped entirely, where she would only wait to die. My time was moving forward in a clear progression: high school, college, law school. Now my years counted for something; they were intended to end in something. They were the antithesis of the long, pointless high school summers with my mother, of their profligate, hopeless waste of hours. I felt I could not step back into my mother's time again, as if it were a quicksand that would keep me.

A FEW DAYS after I visited Sarah, my aunt sent me a letter in which she said that she'd delicately raised the subject of suicide with my mother, asking her if she found her life, as it was, tolerable—in short, whether she wanted sleeping pills to kill herself.

In response, my mother, half aware, said something garbled and almost unintelligible that my aunt interpreted as "What? Take my life?"

Reading the letter, I speculated that my mother actually

might have said "Want to take my life" instead. In my uncertainty, I was reminded of judicial opinions I'd been reading for class about relatives fighting over whether patients in comas who hadn't left behind living wills would have wanted to die. Courts could only infer and speculate, from the person's statements and actions in life, what he or she would have chosen.

I did not want to think of my mother clinging to the shreds of her life, even as the neurons melted within her brain into plaques and tangles. I wanted to believe she would prefer death over this indignity and horror. But I could only guess what she would really have wanted. Like my father, she had become gradually less familiar to me over the years in college and law school, when I had spoken to her only on the phone, until she might almost have been a stranger, until I could no longer confidently say, "That's like her, that's unlike her."

It still hurt me to think about my mother, but I believed that once I had made my decision not to help her I had no right to feel this pain, to claim this grief, because I'd fled from the obligations that had brought with them this right. Instead, I tried to put her out of my mind, to pretend to myself and others that I had a different, untroubled life.

To abandon my mother entirely meant I had to lie. I claimed I stayed at school over vacations to catch up on work after a semester's procrastination, and I generally would not listen to my answering-machine messages in front of anyone else. But once I slipped: Aaron and I were in my dorm room and I had begun to play back messages, to see if a friend had called about dinner, when a bird flew down the fireplace and began banging around the room. As I moved to open the window for the bird, I heard my aunt's voice explaining how sick my mother was, how she'd thrown up in the car when my uncle had visited and they'd tried to take her for a drive. The message was over before I could get to the machine to shut it off.

"Did you know that about your mom?" Aaron asked me, surprised.

"She gets nauseous," I said. I opened the window and the bird left unerringly; in a single straight shot it was gone. "She just can't go on long drives, that's all."

I thought that if Aaron knew about my mother's illness he'd never understand why I didn't at least visit her. I felt sure that I could never explain how I felt so that he would understand. Maybe no one could understand it but me, or maybe I couldn't fully explain it even to myself.

I knew that Aaron was a good son, but it was so easy for him to be one. His mother made pies and cooed at him when he went home to New Canaan on weekends. His father had founded his own computer company and then sold it. His money would see him and his wife through a luxurious retirement. Even though he saw little of his parents, Aaron stayed firmly on the safe side of the social line I'd crossed; how he might confront his parents' eventual illnesses and deaths— how much time he'd take from his law practice, how deeply he might care, whether he might move to be near them—all this was a matter of speculation.

It was not by any means the first time I'd lied to a boy-friend about my mother. Time after time in college I'd dated men but couldn't really fall in love with them—as hard as I tried, as much as they endeared themselves to me. It was as if a match were scraped against a hard surface over and over, rasping insistently but refusing to bloom into light.

Nor could I trust them enough to tell them the truth. Though I'd had the recurring wish to tell, I'd also made the re-peated decision to keep silent. There was one man I'd dated before Aaron whom I was tempted to tell. He was depressive. When we made love, his face beneath mine scrolled through degrees of partial grief, of transient pleasure grafted onto some intractable, permanent sorrow. If anyone could understand, I thought, he could. Yet I did not tell even him.

I think the men I dated could never quite figure me out—rightly, since they were missing several crucial pieces of infor-mation. That my mother was dying, of course. That I felt guilt over having done nothing to help her. But, more than this, that I was strangely inside my mother's death somehow—imprisoned in the invisible cage of it.

Chapter Four

THE SUMMER AFTER my second year of law school, Aaron and I decided to live together in New York City. The city's legal world, at once contentious and insular, seemed incredibly attractive to me. Being good at school could mean doing well at work; doing well at work could mean that I counted in the world, somehow.

New York seemed like the Emerald City itself, where all your requests would be answered. And it was the city of escape, I thought. It had served that function for so many for so long, and it was those like me—the escaped ones, those who had chosen it—I imagined, who loved the city best. It was impersonal, anonymous. People would rarely know your background when they met you. They would not ask about your family, I hoped, not in the searching, interested way that people in the South or the Midwest might. I could say that my mother had died years ago. Or that she lived far away. I could claim that she was alive and well but that we were estranged, so I didn't visit. I could say anything. No one would know the truth.

I remembered a fairy tale I'd read as a child in which a boy could tell anyone's character simply by shaking his hand. Rather than feeling a human palm, he'd feel the wing of a swan, the chain-mail skin of a snake, a pig's cloven hoof, or the terrible hooked wing-end of a bat. You might rack up diamond rings on your fingers or sheathe your hands in gloves, but with his touch these inessential things would vanish and the boy would know your true nature. I reminded myself that people in real life did not have these powers: they could not see in me what was small and selfish and animal, the claws and wings.

The loft Aaron and I were renting was on Jane Street, in the quietest part of the West Village—so far west it was only blocks from the Hudson River, next to the broad streets of the Meat Packing District. The nearby apartment buildings were topped by water towers squat on their crisscrossed metal bases or by roof gardens verdant in the rich summer.

The loft was quiet: the city's noises, its car alarms and insistent sirens and shouted curses, could not be heard there. Aaron mocked what the loft's owners had left behind: Movement posters, progressive children's books, books on Marx and by Marcuse, several early editions of *Our Bodies, Ourselves*, copies of *The Nation* back to 1960. To make his point, he held up a small bust of Lenin and waved it at me, the fierce, elegant goateed head no bigger than his palm.

But I loved the loft instantly, the moment I walked in. The partitions in lieu of interior walls, its oversized scale, larger than human. The door so huge that, when it was open, the apartment lacked an entire section of one of its walls. The clusters of tall potted plants. The woven hangings from South America. The eclectic furniture, some of it grotesquely claw-footed. The way sun came in through the skylights and moved across the apartment slowly, so that the air in the loft seemed viscous with light.

Moving into the loft, I imagined that I felt life opening before us: this apartment that we would share as a couple; my summer law firm job; his studying for the bar. It was a life that would look perfect from the outside—like the model contents of a display dollhouse that was made to be riven, to swing open on a hinge.

The law firm where I worked that summer was housed in a black Park Avenue monolith, many stories up. Aaron had worked for a very similar firm the previous summer and he intended to return now that he had graduated. That summer he would spend studying for the bar, followed by a pleasure trip to Barcelona. In the fall, he would start work while I finished my third and final year of law school.

Aaron was jealous, convinced that the associates at the predominantly male firm—where everyone worked all the time and had little opportunity to meet anyone—would ask me out. I did mention to friends at the firm that I had a boy-friend, as Aaron had asked, but without much enthusiasm or specificity.

In the course of the previous summer, working at a firm had changed Aaron profoundly. Aaron's intelligence was sexy, direct and quick, but it was also scary. It allowed him to adapt so perfectly to the institutions in which he worked; I always thought he would excel in whatever environment he was placed in. The firm had made him the type of young corporate lawyer who revels in the perquisites of his job, living like a vampire off certain bloodless concepts—the prestige of his firm, the design of his suit, the color of his credit card, the ex-pensive restaurants at which he could now afford to lunch. He kept the *Zagat* restaurant guide tucked in an inside pocket of his jacket at all times, as if it were a paperback Bible or as if he were Justice Black carrying a dog-eared copy of the Con-stitution. After I graduated, he wanted us to live together in the Trump Tower. He'd already calculated that, with two law firm salaries, we would be able to afford it.

Aaron sought a life lived according to the cycle of the Deal. The negotiations, the drafting of the final paperwork, the trip to the printer for proofreading. The arranging of the agree-ments on a huge conference table, the signing so that the legal relationships were set, the ordering of caviar and champagne. For the associates, a night of binge drinking and then, finally, tonic sleep, for half a day. Later, the "tombstones" that memorialized the Deal—icons that were small replicas of the client company's products embalmed in plastic—would be distributed. Then, eventually, the next Deal would come.

That summer I was to work on litigation, some of which was connected to deals like those Aaron worked on. I wanted to want this, and I knew at the same time that I did not want it. I was out of place at the firm from the beginning. I entered its world with a strange detachment I could never shake. The legal positions Aaron inhabited—the jobs he became—would be, for me, only impostures, the price of my hiding.

I worked at the firm for a while, mechanically. I wrote memoranda to partners on the interpretation of contract clauses. I researched the requirements for shareholder class actions. I was briefly sent out of state to help with a securities fraud trial.

Then I fell in love. It was someone at the firm, as if Aaron's jealousy had been a prophecy.

When I met Paul Arias he was twenty-eight, a year younger than I am now. He wore glasses made of a light, yellowy tortoiseshell, with an extra bar between the lenses. He has strong cheekbones but there is a softness to his face, too; his expression is naturally inquisitive. He is rapacious, feral in a way. In his smile, his subtly pointed canine teeth show, and their sharpness emphasizes his slight widow's peak. His fingers are gentle, careful and long and thin. Standing, he holds his hips canted in a slightly feminine way. When I met him, his slight eccentricities and his irreverent carriage seemed doubly odd in the setting of the firm.

Aaron has the kind of intelligence one can see immediately in the eyes, the alertness of a bright child: a light, a quickness. By contrast, Paul's eyes have a caginess, an opacity. I learned from him that I liked this closed handsomeness much more.

My crush started at a firm event at a Spanish restaurant in the West Village. When I'd left the office that evening, short on sleep, my eyes were closing without my volition, but as soon as I began speaking with Paul, I found that I was full of adrenaline. I had noticed him before, had asked his name. That night he reached me somehow, through my autopilot life, my walking trance. At the restaurant, I drank, though I usually did not, pouring the sangria liberally through its mess of fruit. There was a prettier woman there—but he spoke to me instead. I felt sexualized in his presence, as if there were an invisible film of electric static on my skin that would separate into a blue circle of light around a finger if it were breached by touch.

When he walked me home through cobbled, deserted streets to the loft, I dared to kiss him there, although I knew Aaron was waiting upstairs for me to come home. I loved kissing him, finding in it a certain pricey freedom of the heart.

"Can I see your apartment?" he asked. "I hear it's great."

"Not tonight," I told him.

"Do you live with someone?"

"I have a roommate. He's probably asleep. We'd wake him up. There aren't really walls."

He shrugged. "Another time then." He kissed me again.

It was enthralling, the beginning of the risk of this affair. For him, too: I knew he was more intrigued because he sensed there was a good reason I could not ask him upstairs. The transgression was sexy for him, I could tell.

We were a good match in treachery, it turned out. I soon found out from other associates at the firm that, like me, Paul was seeing someone seriously—a woman named Angela whom he'd dated ever since college, who was pressuring him to marry her. And I learned later that we were both, then, the type of people who could not leave well enough alone, contrarians of love and sex; the type of people compelled to do heedless damage to others, as if by some emotional injunction.

Paul and I made a dinner date almost immediately, to go out for Indian food at one of the many restaurants on Sixth Street between First and Second Avenues.

"It's the most efficient market in New York," he'd commented on the phone, suggesting it. "Waiters from another restaurant will come and solicit you while you're waiting in line."

I dressed up for too long beforehand, in sheer anxiety. By

the time I got there, my separate eyelashes stood apart like a doll's, heavy with too many coats of mascara.

When we met on Sixth Street he said at once, "I need to go back to my apartment and get my wallet. It's a few blocks away."

"No problem," I replied. "I'd love to see your apartment anyway."

He looked nervous, walking with me on the street, past the balding parks of the East Village. I could tell he felt strongly that he walked in risk. He put the collar of his jacket up around his ears and hunched down, as if that would keep him from getting caught. I walked dreamily beside him, looking up at the buildings. The most beautiful architecture of the city, it seemed to me, was also the most distant: a tower suffused with light, or adorned with a great clock ringed in neon.

Paul's East Village apartment was small, a single room with a casketlike bedchamber in a raised loft. In one corner, brown plastic crates were stacked on top of one another like the skeletons of soft-cornered children's blocks. Next to them were bookshelves, with framed photos on the top shelves. One photo was of a woman I knew must be his girlfriend, Angela. Her hair was white-blonde, with strands the color of the strings that remain on a husked corncob. She wore a white blouse with a dull, nacreous shine.

Paul picked up his wallet from a table near the door, but neither of us made a motion to leave.

I felt oddly as if nothing went on outside that room, ever had, ever would. I identified the room at once as the stage, the central place, of my life: where what would matter would happen. Being there with Paul was freeing; it was like a separate, safe world. There, I was not the person I was in life: whom her parents had left mostly alone, who had left her mother alone later, who ought to go back, who ought to work harder, who would always strain and never be at peace. And unlike Aaron, Paul wasn't supposed to know about my family, so there wouldn't be any issue of concealing things from him, of lying.

After a few moments, Paul took his coat off. Under it he wore a white T-shirt, tight enough that it was evident his chest was well shaped, but not skintight. He had on old jeans with white patches where frayed threads showed through, taut and parallel as if in a sewing kit, and black cowboy boots with stitching. I had begun to want him viscerally, as I had not known I could want someone.

"We shouldn't see each other," I said.

"We shouldn't," he agreed. "You should leave right now," he added softly.

Then he reached toward me to touch me for the first time, to first establish his access to my body, gathering my hair at the back of my neck, then gently touching the wisps that strayed. I stood very still for him to do this.

"I'm so attracted to you," he said. "You're a little sexy

when you dress for work, you know. There's something insincere about your wearing a suit. Like it's not really you, just something you're affecting for the moment."

"That's how I feel about it," I admitted, "as if I'm impersonating a lawyer."

I slipped away from him for a moment to look at his bookshelves, picked up a novel I liked. I was stalling for time. I knew there was still a way to leave graciously, to maneuver us out to Sixth Street for dinner. I needed this fiercely, afraid of it and wanting it. But I kept telling myself that, up to the very last moment, the choice was mine. We could just have dinner; that was what we had planned to do, after all.

"What do you think of this?" I asked.

"It's Angela's," he said. "My girlfriend. I only read history, not fiction. Usually ancient."

"Ancient history," I pointed out, "is *like* fiction. It has no relevance to your life. Like the expression 'That's ancient history.'"

"At least someone's willing to claim it's true," he countered.

We bantered more. Neither of us really listened to the conversation.

Then he came very close to me, to let me know we were starting.

But I was the one who began it. I took his T-shirt off; he raised his arms straight up like a little boy to let me. I couldn't help noticing the flatness of his stomach, the tautness of his hairless chest, smooth as plastic. It seemed to me that there were two kinds of skin: mine—slightly pink and seemingly ready to bloom into fat at any moment I was less than vigilant; and his—a thin, flawless overlay directly atop muscle and bone. His body seemed as if it would always be the same. He never exercised, but it was perfect anyway. It had probably looked the same when he was twenty; I thought that when he was forty, it would look just this way.

I found that I was delighted to undress him, that I had been dying to do it. His muscles were smooth and long. His feet and hands were oddly delicate. There was something eerie about the handsomeness of his body, strangely fluid, as if he'd slip into places you wouldn't want him to go, escape you if you tried to hold him.

We started touching, rolling around on the couch. At some point we moved up to his narrow loft bed, where one could not stand upright—clambering up there on the ladder.

"I suppose Indian food was a bit of a euphemism," he said as we climbed.

He was hard to me then, at the beginning, touching me hard and reactively, with pressure and without tenderness. Kissing me, he let his teeth catch slightly at the edge of my lip. He subtly bit the soft skin of my earlobes, too, the points of his teeth making impressions like pinpoints, like the beginning of ear piercing in the moment before the bolt is shot through. He bit me on my upper arms and shoulders: just hard enough to bruise slightly. When I sat up in bed, he pushed me down to kiss me, pressing the heels of his hands into the soft pads of flesh directly beneath my collarbone, like an animal pinning another down.

I wondered later if this harshness initially emphasized the simple physicality of our being together for him, reassured him as to its hollowness beneath the skin. If it clarified for him, at every moment, that his heart was elsewhere.

"All this high school bump-and-grind really brings you to a pitch," he said.

A moment later, we started having sex. He began to labor above me, under a film of sweat; I moved with him. I was spaced out with pleasure, entirely there and entirely gone at the same time. Then I was above him, my hair falling around him, clinging to itself in bunches like the threads of a feather. He held it aside to see my eyes.

It was over quickly; his motions speeded into spasms and he came inside me, while my own arousal was still unlocalized, uncoordinated, while I was still dreamy.

Afterward, I sat naked on top of the sheet, knees tucked to my chest, arms locked around my legs, my stomach creased in the center of the ball my body made: like a carapaced beetle prompted by touch to curl up into a sphere. Near me, Paul lay freely, stretched out, sexy, his head resting on the pad of his interlocked fingers so that his elbows made triangular spaces.

Looking into the extreme blue of his eyes, I felt a small mental discontinuity, a little jolt of intense surprise at what I had done so impulsively, with so little reflection. The feeling of betrayal came to me only then. I had put off this admission as long as possible; I'd convinced myself, up until the moment we kissed, that I might simply have dinner with Paul, an innocent thing. Then sex had been an impetuous slide, unstoppable. Now I had no choice but to face this. I thought of Aaron alone in the loft, studying, expecting me to come home at any moment. I had told him I was having dinner with Sarah—she'd moved to the city and was teaching French again, at a prep school on the Upper West Side.

My first affair, I thought. It seemed an end to any innocence that remained in me. It seemed to open the door to many other possible betrayals (and maybe, I speculate now, the betrayal of my mother had opened the door to this). I would know, from now on, that this was possible. A limit, passed, had disappeared. The change felt sad, like the loss of hope. And it felt as if it would have consequences, like the flagrant breaking of the law.

Sitting beside Paul, I willed him to touch me. But I also knew that he couldn't, not now. It would be unthinkable to him, ruinous to our affair. It would infringe on some right of Angela's. After sex, his body was his own; he would not comfort me with it. And, returned to himself after sex, he was as uneasy as I was, with much the same guilt.

"Everything will be fine," he said carelessly. "You don't need to be upset. Why are you so upset?"

"I'm not," I lied, shaking my head miserably.

"Are you worried we'll get caught?" he asked. "By your boyfriend or someone? Come on, don't worry. I won't say a thing to anyone. We're too smart for that. People like us don't get caught."

"People like you don't," I corrected him.

WHEN I CAME home, Aaron was taking a shower. The spray clouded the bathroom with scent and steam that drifted over the partition into the rest of the loft, swirling like smoke, fuming like dry ice. I slipped into the shower room to see Aaron. The small room seemed even more intimate in comparison to the huge loft. It was clean and white-tiled, with faded caulking. It smelled of oranges.

I watched as, through the transparent curtain, the outline of Aaron's body became progressively blurrier and its color appeared to change. He was shimmering out, the lines that marked the edges of his limbs softening. I felt for a second as if I were seeing him in another world, an evanescent place of ectoplasm and mist—the world of the dead. I felt how close by that world was, how time could unveil it.

I stepped into the shower next to Aaron, as if in a moment I could wash away my time with Paul. He held me with his chin grazing the top of my head. His cheeks were covered with the bluish cast of a dark stubble, as they always were by that time of night. The nozzle's warm, uneven stream of water struck his body first; I shrank away from the cold air toward him, touching him with my thighs, my forearms, the wet flats of my palms, as if the heat derived directly from him. Standing there, with his larger body protecting mine, I knew that the emotion I felt for him was a bit slight and small, disappointing and gentle. Yet it seemed to me that this quiet, limited affection—you could ignore for years, maybe forever, the compromises it implied—might be the emotion that came with safety. Still, I did not have it in me to choose it.

After showering, I sat with him on the bed. My damp hair lay in tendrils on my neck. Fat drops of water slipped down the separate strands, then flicked off the tips, melting into the bed. I knew I did not feel enough, did not feel love. And I knew that in time I would leave him, as I had left everyone so far. I knew, too, that the leaving would feel familiar and comfortable, as if leaving were the choice of my one true self, and every commitment, that self's betrayal.

THAT SUMMER, MY aunt Betty began to send me letters and packages at the loft—as if she imagined that the objects would build up, gradually and insidiously, and with their collective presence shame me into visiting my mother.

First, my aunt sent me a set of the nursing home's reports. My mother, the reports said, was frequently incontinent. She would laugh without any reason. She couldn't see well enough to cut her food and she had trouble chewing. She walked stooped over and with difficulty. She couldn't fit her room key into its keyhole; she'd fumble with it for a long time, then begin to cry.

Later, my aunt sent me a card signed by my mother in a scrawl—a loosening of my mother's former signature, the loops of the letters flattening and opening out. The signature would have been illegible if I hadn't already known it must say "Mom."

With the card, Betty also enclosed a photo. In it, my mother, weighing over two hundred pounds, wears a sweatshirt, sweatpants, and slippers: clothes my aunt bought, the only ones that fit. A man sits next to her, leathery-faced. My aunt had mentioned him: "He's your mother's knight in shining armor," she'd said. "He does everything, cuts her meat for her, escorts her around. He's a born-again, a little crazy, but I don't know what she'd do without him."

In the photo, my mother holds a squat glass filled with ice and scotch or gin—a present from my aunt, even though (or because) she is an alcoholic. Her lipstick smeared and uneven, she laughs toward the camera. Her filled cavities are visible, as dark spots, in the gape of her laugh. It reminded me of how, yelling or laughing, my mother always let her voice go, didn't check herself, how she vented her emotion on the world, mouth open.

She is laughing mostly to herself, off in her own world. Her eyes don't focus on the camera. A deep haze, of alcohol and of disease, has set in. How much does she know, as she is dying?

That dazed laugh: maybe, I thought fleetingly, the disease made my mother unaware of the full magnitude of her situation. This was my aunt's hope, but I could never believe it. I thought her mind must have watched itself die; I thought she knew all the time.

I tried to keep the photo, the card, and the reports in the loft, but I couldn't settle on a hiding place for them. Anywhere I put them, it seemed that Aaron might come across them. Then I tried to throw them out, but every time I crumpled the photo, its stiff cardboard backing kept opening to display its slick colors. Finally, I threw away everything my aunt had sent, burying it in several plastic bags and leaving it in a public trash can several blocks away from the loft.

I wondered, if someone else saw the photo, what that person would think. The woman in the photo could have been someone's sad grandmother—but she was not, she was my mother, prematurely aged, struck with a disease of the old in her late forties. I envied the stranger who could come upon the photo and not know what it meant, who would not recognize the woman who sits, holding her drink with both hands, on a cheap couch covered in nubbly plaid in a nursing home in the state where she will die, far from the places where she grew up and lived, without any family but her sister to attend her. I knew I was not quite this stranger yet—a person who could look at this photograph unmoved and only curious. But I still hoped I could become such a stranger, with time.

MY AFFAIR WITH Paul began at the very end of June, as the summer was shifting into heat that was like a light gel you walked in. Aaron was scheduled to take the bar in a few weeks. It was after this that I planned to leave him. A few days later, he would leave for his Barcelona vacation and I'd be free: a clean break. And mostly painless—for me, at least. So I procrastinated, putting off the time when I'd have to leave him and using the date of the bar exam as a convenient deadline. At the time, I thought I was procrastinating because I still cared for Aaron in some ways, or at least because I was protecting him from being so upset that he'd fail the bar. Once that summer, a man I knew asked me out, and when I told him, "I'm seeing someone pretty seriously," I found that I felt oddly faithful to both Paul and Aaron at the same time.

But I realized later that what was keeping me from leaving Aaron was not love at all, or even affection. And it wasn't fear of hurting him, not really. Instead, it was mostly a strange inertia—the frozenness I had often felt when my aunt called upon me to come help my mother. I couldn't bear either to forgo what I had chosen or to face its full consequences. And maybe it was more (and more selfish): I think I also feared at some level that, unattached, I might scare Paul away. I knew

Paul would feel a new, abstract demand if I left Aaron, even if I assured him nothing had changed between us. The fact that Paul and I were both cheating put us in equipoise, ensured that we could continue on as we were.

Having made my decision not to leave Aaron for a few weeks, I knew that I had to conceal my relationship with Paul as best I could. The fact that Paul worked in my office was no impediment: he barely met my eyes there and our intimacy was far from apparent.

But once I couldn't resist going into his office. His chair was turned to the window. I surprised him by walking up behind him and resting my hands lightly on his shoulders so that my fingers touched the sides of his neck. Small touches like this still stirred me.

He shrugged out from under my hands gently, sitting up straighter in his chair. Then he swiveled around to face me.

Maybe we would have kissed; maybe he would have chastised me. But his secretary walked in then and just as quickly walked out, and that was enough to caution me forever about such conduct at work.

After that, pretending we were strangers wasn't hard at all, I found. Paul would call from his office to mine to make plans with me, but we would not even stand together in the hall talking. Sometimes we'd share a Dial Car one of us had called —a black, expensive car with a hired driver, a perk for working late—but we wouldn't walk out together. Instead, whichever one of us slipped into the car first would scrunch down a bit and wait for the other.

With Aaron, I became a profligate liar, sacrificing truth for time in order to meet Paul at the last minute. After a while, lying to Aaron became almost a challenge. Explaining where I'd been, or explaining away signs of my distraction, I'd race around in my thoughts frenetically, culling them, trying to skim as close to the truth as possible so that later I wouldn't constantly have to lie just to be consistent. It was like the practice of law, I realized: an enterprise of justification in retrospect. After the fact, I would construct an explanation, consistent with all the evidence, that could have been true.

Often when I wanted to see Paul I told Aaron I'd be at the office but unreachable, in a meeting in one of the conference rooms or in the firm's library. The lawyers for whom I worked were my unknowing accomplices in these deceptions; the firm's reputation for keeping its associates working all the time, including evenings and weekends, ensured that every excuse was plausible. In the evening, I would often notice older associates, almost all male and single, having a late dinner together in a conference room, and I'd think of Melville's term for the society of lawyers: the paradise of bachelors. This paradise of bachelors would, ironically, protect my affair. I did work a lot. Work seemed merely like time spent in limbo, penance that had to be paid for bliss. Since I could see Paul only rarely, why not work? But I also frequently used work as an excuse.

Sometimes I would even call Aaron from Paul's apartment and lie to him about where I was—constructing alibis while Paul held me in his lap, locking his arms around my waist; keeping my voice steady even as he kissed the side of my neck, nuzzling into it against my chin's protest. It troubled me surprisingly little to lie so much. Being with Paul felt so imperative that it didn't seem I had a choice in the matter. For a while everything seemed fine. If I did not claim to be at work, I claimed to be with Sarah. She promised to cover for me. And it seemed Aaron believed my lies.

Still, I knew I'd have to sleep with Aaron sooner or later or he'd become suspicious—I couldn't claim to be tired forever. But I was scared that somehow he'd figure out, in bed, that I had been unfaithful. I finally chose a time late at night, when he probably wouldn't be very observant. We kissed on the couch. Eventually we trooped to the bedroom. Aaron swatted me companionably on the butt as I undressed.

During the act, because I felt nothing, it seemed as if I were peculiarly observant, as if I saw Aaron especially clearly. Since he'd graduated, he'd stopped playing rugby and tennis, started going out more in the city, and gradually acquired an inflection of fat at his otherwise thin waist: a semisoft band of flesh that encircled his waist like an ill-fitting belt, the sediment of some habit of eating or drinking. As he thrust into me, I felt that I touched him only mediately—as one might, holding a tissue, pick up something with distaste. I might have been able to find a belly endearing, but this circle of flesh repelled me.

He thrust away; I could not move with his motion, tried in vain.

While he was inside me, he reached down to touch me, and I came, but I couldn't meet his eyes. He knew me so well that it was almost routine for him to do this. I'd been grateful for it before, but now I almost hated him for it: he could make me come without my wanting to, in a physical reaction as involuntary as retching, as meaningless as a yawn. As I came, I fought down the urge to cry.

Afterward, in that moment after coming where desire itself seems impossible, implausible, I felt a deep indifference—toward Aaron and toward myself—and the beginning of despair. I thought about how Aaron could make me come so easily and how I never could come with Paul. I suspected that it was another thing Paul kept from me, like all the information about his friends and family he wouldn't tell me—something he'd reserved for Angela. When he was aroused, he'd speed our rhythm, withdrawing well before I could get close to coming. Sometimes his timing seemed almost malicious, but I could never be sure. I didn't like receiving oral sex—that level of vulnerability and exposure felt far too high to me—and he never offered. So our sex was like a piece of music played over and over, yet always, at the same point, interrupted—so that one could only imagine, from the patterns and refrains, how it would end. An endlessly deferred pleasure —perhaps that was what drew me to Paul. A promise that, as hard as I tried, I'd never really know him, that he'd always partially resist me.

That night Aaron and I did not speak very much before we fell asleep; our recounting of our days had become cursory. Like his body, Aaron's mind seemed used up to me now, repellent, unable to evoke the pleasure it once had.

Asleep next to Aaron, I dreamt that I was walking up Park Avenue, flanked by two lawyers from the firm, gesturing to explain a legal point—my summer suit immaculate, my hair up, my blocky heels clicking on the pavement.

Next to a corporate fountain, its arcs of water timed into an orchestrated rise and fall, a woman crouched. Her visible flesh was marked by open sores. She was mired in the fluids of her body, that decaying body her only home. With both hands she held a paper bag crunched to narrow into pleats around a bottle's neck.

Without stopping, one of the other lawyers leaned down for a second to give her money, a dollar bill. As she reached up to take it, her ragged sleeves slipping down her arms, I realized it was my mother.

She met my eyes, recognized me, but said nothing.

I did not miss a word of my legal explanation as I walked past.

I woke from the dream suddenly but kept still. I wished I were alone, so I wouldn't have to lie still to hide this fear, this sudden awakening, from Aaron. My mouth tasted of salt; I wondered if I'd been crying in my sleep. If I had, Aaron had not heard me. He was still sleeping peacefully by my side, sweet looking in a wrinkled T-shirt, his eyes closed into slight curves, his lips spittled at one corner, his hair tousled, his face supremely innocent.

I TOLD THE cabdriver Paul's address. I always loved the anticipation of the heady cab ride over to Paul's—its suspension of time, my early arousal.

"A pretty girl like you has a boyfriend, right?" The cabdriver's Russian accent was subtle, lovely. He kept glancing at me in the rearview mirror.

"Yes, but I'm actually going to see another guy." I smiled into the mirror coyly, as if my cheating were a joke between us, so tired of lying that I casually told the truth.

The cabdriver stiffened and turned the music up. He avoided my eyes in the mirror.

Pictures of his wife and four children were affixed to the dashboard. The cab was uncomfortable, beat up, with slits in the forest green seats spilling out dirty foam and a lingering smell of smoke. The rope of wooden beads behind the driver's back was partially torn in two.

Silently I looked out the window at the ads on the six-foot-tall lighted plates on the sides of phone booths and bus stops. My skirt slipped to the side for a moment to show the fluted edge of my stocking, the beginning of the garter belt's architecture, and I quickly corrected it.

When I tried to pay the cabdriver, he wouldn't take my money.

"No, no. You keep it," he said. "You are going to need it."

He peeled away the moment I was out of the cab, so fast I almost tripped as I was closing the door.

The doorman buzzed Paul and then waved me upstairs. He seemed curious about who I was to Paul. He must have seen Angela all the time.

Paul opened the door, half grinning; I'd found he had a variety of half smiles and faraway looks. He held up a hand, indicating that I should be quiet. He was on the phone with his parents, who were both well-known Boston lawyers. I listened intently: if he'd known how hard I listened to everything he ever said, he would have been unnerved. He seemed to have a xenophobically close family that coexisted, without much expressiveness, in a sort of assumed but unconditional love. I suppose it goes without saying that I was jealous.

"How's your family?" I asked after he hung up.

"Fine," he said curtly.

"Was your father teasing you about being arrogant again?" I asked. It had seemed that way.

"You're not supposed to remember that," he replied, rueful and somewhat surprised. He began to kiss me then, I think in order to quiet me, but I squirmed away from his kiss.

I wanted to talk; I always tried, but it bored or threatened him.

"Do you think we have an odd relationship?" I asked him.

"No, I think we have a normal affair. I think we're corrupt in an ordinary way."

He smiled, looking for approval, for me to think him funny. He addressed my questions squarely, without being comforting. Paul was exactly fair to me and no more, I realized.

We rarely spoke about work or friends and when we did it seemed artificial. The only thing that seemed natural for us was to have sex: it was really all we did together well. I wanted more, of course. I wanted to know him. I wanted to pry open his hard breastplate and see the heart inside. I wanted to know where the life inside him lived. Not just the details, the trivia of it, but more: to know how it felt to him to live it.

So I extrapolated, embellished from the few things I knew, building intricate castles of logic in thin evidentiary air like the lawyer I was halfway to becoming. It was profoundly lonely to learn about him. No one could correct me in my apocrypha, my reinterpretations. Nor could anyone confirm for me the things I thought were true. Sometimes I would review my memories of our nights in his apartment sequentially—as if I were walking back through a train of linked, separate boxcars, dispassionately examining the room and its occupants to try to draw conclusions about them. There were small differences among the rooms that I imagined passing through: in one, a champagne bottle and empty glasses sitting abandoned on a table; in another, a photo album that was open, so I could look. Emotionally there were small differences too, degrees of hope and loss.

That night, things proceeded as they always did. I bowed my head to him so he could pull over it the wide loop of the silver chain I wore, as if it were a mantle. He detached the backs of my earrings and gently pulled them out. Then he took off my blouse and skirt. I was right that the garter belt I had so riskily put on did not surprise him in the least. I thought that women must dress up like this for Paul, that it was somehow necessary.

He loved the play of exposing my body slowly. He always wanted me at first to wear nothing at all while he remained fully dressed, like the nude in *Déjeuner sur l'herbe*. Then he would condescend to undress himself.

Once undressed, we moved upstairs to the raised warren where he slept. I lay down, resting my head on one of my hands. He traced a line from the soft, stretched skin of my underarm, the tiny points of hair just visible, to the curve beneath my breast.

He said, into my neck, "Isn't it amazing that we want this so much?"

When we started having sex, I gripped his back tightly at the sides with my thighs. For a moment, I touched my feet together behind his back to better grip him. He reached behind my back to grab the two large, flat bones of my shoulders, as if he could press them together and make me open for him farther. I wanted to open for him, as far as I could. He found his way deeper inside me.

Then the phone rang out in a long trill. We both tensed in spasms. I slid out from under him immediately. I scrambled nervously backward and away from him, as if we'd been caught together, crab-walking on the flats of my hands. I thought of Aaron at his desk, with his deadeningly dull bar books piled high.

The pauses in the ringing seemed like breaths, like the spaces between an animal's howling.

"I'm not going to get it," Paul said. "The machine will pick up."

The phone kept ringing. Despite this, Paul entered me again. The few moments of sex felt bizarre and crooked, scrapy and large-eyed and harsh. He came inside me almost immediately.

After a few more rings, Angela's voice filled the room as she left a message. Paul pulled out.

"Where are you, darling?" Her voice was high but strong. "I thought you would be home by now. Love you. Call me."

She was a cipher to me. I couldn't imagine their being college classmates, their shared vacations, the introductions to his family, and the fights, pressure from her toward marriage and his resistance. What if she found out about me and confronted me someday? Would we arch away from each other like cats? Spite would be there, but it would be matched by a strange, serious curiosity, lingering in our faces, about what we had in common and the different things Paul wanted us for. We had something to say to each other; we must.

When the machine clicked off, Paul was monkey-faced, sullen, stiff in obvious discomfort.

"Why do you stay with her?" I asked him.

He shrugged. "The question is more, why do I cheat on her? I love her, in some ways. I don't think I want to marry her. Not now, anyway." He paused.

"Why do you stay with Aaron?" he asked. "Do you love him?"

"No," I said. "I'm not in love."

"That," he said, "was what I thought."

Before I left, while he was out of the room, I surreptitiously dropped one of my earrings, a small pearl on a wire, between the cushions of his couch, leaving it for Angela to find: a clue. And I spritzed the couch with a hint of my perfume. I thought of deer leaving trails in the woods for each other to follow, marking twigs with fluid from dark crevices next to their eyes.

"I DON'T REALLY feel comfortable seeing you and Aaron together, Julie," Sarah complained. "I feel like I'm making a fool of him because I know about Paul."

"I have to see him tonight," I told her. "I've canceled on him too many times recently. I'd like to see you, too."

"Why don't you just break up with Aaron now? You know you want to do it eventually."

"It'll be easier for him after the bar."

"You should just be honest now. He'll be fine. It's not like you have a perfect relationship. He knows that. It would be better."

"I'll do it soon. I just don't want to do it now."

"Can you at least not ask me to cover for you so much?" she asked. "It makes me nervous."

"Okay," I said. "But I might need you, sometimes."

"What's going on with you and Paul?" she asked me.

"I don't see him that often," I lied. "I like him a lot. Maybe we'll go out at the end of the summer."

"Does he know about Aaron?"

"He has an idea."

"It doesn't bother him?"

"He knows it won't go on that long. I need to go, a partner wants me to come to his office," I lied a second time. "Will you please come tonight?"

"Okay," she agreed. I gave her directions.

My life had become so complex and shameful that I felt I couldn't trust anyone with the entire story of it—even Sarah. But I realized how much I missed talking to her honestly, the way we had in college. Then it had seemed that we bolstered each other in some vital way. We told each other everything. And we each had an assumption of the other's basic worth and talent that we could never fully apply to ourselves.

Now I was becoming less honest with Sarah. She knew I had decided not to live near my mother in Tucson, but she did not know about my mother's full decline. She did not know—though she might have guessed—that I did not even visit.

Sarah's own mother was getting better; she was less depressed, less crazy. Her father was carefully taking care of her mother, although it took its toll on him. And Sarah visited her parents more often than she had. They were just a subway ride away, in Brooklyn Heights, and she could easily retreat to her own apartment afterward. Sometimes she'd go have coffee with her father alone and let him complain about her mother until he felt better. There were still problems: Sarah herself suffered from depression, rarely dated, lacked sex drive, she told me. But in other ways her life had naturally begun to resolve itself. She had left as I had, made her break with her family when she'd gone to college, but then she had come back, an independent person, for a reconciliation. As it seemed that everyone did—except me.

What happened with Sarah and her family was the way things were supposed to happen: the natural separation, then the reunion. It was only I, it seemed, who lived in the breach always, who would never feel it seal. I was the only one left still in rebellion, as if I had broken my curfew one night as a teenager and never returned to be punished by my parents, and yet to have them confess that they loved me, that they had worried. As each day passed, I diverged farther from the normal path even as Sarah returned to it. Soon she would be just as other people were. Their world would easily welcome her back, even as I became a greater outcast in it, a more complete impostor.

SARAH AND I met Aaron at a Jamaican bar in the West Village, its atmosphere raucous, joyful and loud. On the wall, loin-clothed wooden figures beat loudly on taut cloth drums, their arms moved by strings and pulleys.

I was still dressed for work in a severe black suit, but I had switched my work earrings for a pair Sarah had made for me: upside-down silver cups from India rimmed with bells that jangled and rustled tinily. As I walked to the bar, their ringing was barely audible to me, like some small, in-decipherable reminder or sign.

Sarah wore a black vintage top from the twenties covered with sequins and beads, and well-faded Levi's. Her shoulders were so thin that it seemed as though her top hung from a coat hanger. The extra height of her high heels in combination with the taper of her jeans made her legs into mosquito legs — long stalks in which her calves were only slight inflections. A neurotic-looking girl, her dark hair a frizzy corona that needed taming, Sarah was messily beautiful nonetheless. Un-controversially so, with wide-set eyes and an open face like a child's. She was stared at as we jostled through the crowd to-ward a table in the back. Feeling plain next to her, I freed my hair so it fell to my shoulders, keeping my elasticized hair band around my wrist.

"Hey," Aaron said when he arrived there, greeting both of us. "Heeey. You both look great."

I could tell he was in a good mood. He appreciated every break from his studying, and he was just in his element at bars. He visibly brightened at the prospect of them—the gimmickry of Lucy's Surf Bar, the Shark Bar, Le Bar Bat. The quick up-and-down movement of men's eyes as a woman entered. The banter. The beautiful New York women, their black bra tops exposed by open denim shirts, bare-heeled in mules. Aaron was faithful to me, as far as I knew, but he always subtly reminded me of his sacrifices, that he might be entitled by his talents to more, might be entitled to models.

"Let's get drunk," Aaron said. "It's Friday."

As I frequently did, I declined, remembering my mother's tower of bottles. "I have to work tomorrow morning," I said. "I need to finish a memo this weekend." But I was hypocritical: I would drink with Paul, anytime he wanted.

"One drink?"

"I can't."

"Sarah?" he asked.

She looked toward me to see if it was okay, then nodded.

Aaron began to order rounds. Straight shots for him. Seltzer for me. For Sarah, daiquiris filled with thin shards of ice, yellow monkeys hanging precariously by their curled tails from the glass's edge, and later cleanser blue margaritas with plastic sharks submerged among the ice cubes—their gray, back-slanted fins alone visible until Aaron laid one on the table to reveal its thin gills, its white bared teeth.

I went to the jukebox, lingering there at its rainbow neon arch, and chose a song I knew Paul liked—Elvis's "Burning Love"—forcing my access of memory. Listening to the song, or seeing a movie he'd seen, it was as if I cheated the clock, spending more time with him than my current, precious, precarious allotment. I kept a list of all the times I saw him and read it over, describing each meeting to myself, as if that way I could freeze the small spans of time that had begun to make up the heart, the true core, of my life into memory, where they would not be lost. Were it not for these strategies of remembering, my time with Paul would not have been enough; the rarity, the scarcity of it would have been intolerable.

When I returned to the table, Sarah was explaining her college thesis on the poet James Merrill to Aaron. Even after a few drinks, she was very articulate on Merrill, one of her favorite topics. She was born for poetry, I thought to myself: the extension of interior sensibility. And Merrill's work was as delicate and elegant as her ideals of her body and mind were, as delicate and elegant as her vision of her self and life.

"Modern poetry is basically unintelligible," Aaron said. "You shouldn't have to have a doctorate to get it. I can't really believe it makes sense to anyone."

I was about to defend Sarah's work, but she spoke first, more gently than I would have.

"Oh, you would understand it, I think, if you read a whole book of Merrill's," Sarah replied mildly, encouragingly. "One poem teaches you to read the next one. I'll lend you a book if you want," she offered.

Something in Aaron attracted her, I realized. Perhaps in his arrogance he connoted success itself: male effectiveness, mastery of the practical worlds of economics and the law—worlds so foreign to her world of literature and academia. For her part, Sarah must have struck Aaron as fascinatingly ethereal, a fairy-tale creature beyond money.

They ordered their fourth round. Straightening her beaded top, Sarah pulled it down slightly, exposing the beginning of the curve of her breasts for Aaron. She slid her chair closer to his and touched his shoulder casually, to emphasize a point.

"I've bored you to tears, haven't I?" she apologized. "You get me on this topic and I just go on and on."

"I'm sorry, Julie," she added. "I know you've heard this a million times. Are you sure you wouldn't like a drink?" she asked me. "Even a decaf or something?"

I was about to shake my head, but the waitress came over and Sarah quickly ordered drinks for herself and Aaron without waiting for me to respond.

"Okay, let's go," Aaron said finally after they'd finished the last round. It was after one. He quickly put his Gold Card down on top of the check.

"Sarah, we'll walk you home," he announced.

He walked beside me out of the bar, steering Sarah as she walked ahead of us, his hand on her bare shoulder, forcing her to part the crowd more aggressively than she would have liked.

At first all three of us walked together, almost filling the sidewalk so people had to dodge us. Strong smells replaced each other as we walked: of Chinese food, of urine, of burning incense from a street vendor's table. Then Aaron slipped a few paces behind Sarah and me, almost giving us a moment to talk, but before we could say anything he quickly moved behind Sarah and lifted her into the air.

"Aaron!" she screamed.

"You don't weigh anything," he said, slightly surprised. I knew he was mentally comparing her weight to mine.

People eddied around them on the busy avenue. He kept holding her there. In his arms, she was like a put-upon cat, a thin Siamese pulled up under its armpits and left to dangle over a human arm: paws projecting unnaturally, head scrunched too low, legs swinging free, slightly discomfited but the center of attention. Her breasts were pressed up close to her chest, so that the dangling beading of her top skimmed the small hairs on Aaron's forearms as he held her up.

"You know, I could just hold you here," he pointed out, leaning back casually.

Sarah fought him playfully, kicking ineffectually at his legs.

I turned to look at the people on the sidewalk, missing Paul acutely. One of the men passing by gave Aaron an encouraging look. I was bored. I wondered coldly if I could simply give Sarah over to Aaron, if I would lose anything in doing that. There would be a painful realignment, with a question of which connections among us could be maintained.

Sarah looked toward me. I could see in her face that my distraction bothered her. She wanted me to react to this, not to simply, automatically plan around it. I had become so expert at loss, at maintaining the fiction that it was acceptable. It was as if I could lose Sarah, for so long my best friend, in a blink, a second. She knew me, knew that—that I was an adept at quick divorce, that I had the dubious, valuable skill of leaving. Maybe she was testing me with this flirtation. I think if she'd said something to me then, everything would have been different.

Instead she started to fight sincerely against Aaron's grip. Finally she got down from him abruptly, as if slipping off a ledge. Her ankles buckled for a moment. Then her very high heels righted themselves smoothly on the dirty West Village street. She backed away from both of us a few steps.

"I have to go," she said to both of us. "You should go home. It's late."

"You put me in this situation," she whispered to me defensively as she air-kissed me good night. "I'm sorry," she hissed at me, loud enough for Aaron to hear.

She said good night to Aaron rapidly and kept walking, at

a fast clip. Touching Aaron had seemed to be too much for her, as if she'd needed to flee it.

"She okay?" Aaron asked, as if puzzled.

He put his hand at the small of my back as boyfriends do and we walked home as if nothing had happened.

At home I thought of Sarah. Undeniably beautiful though she was, she had not really been with anyone since her dream boyfriend in junior year of college—the handsome son of a famous Italian filmmaker. She did date a lot, but the relationships never lasted long. She'd go out to dinner with men, but she never ate, not really, maintaining some equilibrium, a self-perpetuating system: her lovely thinness, the way clothes fell on her, made these men want to take her to dinner, but when they did, she barely ate. I think she spooked the men she dated with the seeming brittleness of her body, her uneven, high voice, her discursive manner of speaking. She seemed a creature of small bottles, of liqueurs and perfumes, of stoppered unguents. She connoted hysteria and early sorrow. They would sleep with her, but she was not the steady girlfriend they wanted.

As I undressed for bed, I took off the earrings she'd made for me, placing them on the dresser. Gingerly, I touched one of my bare earlobes—deep-slitted from wearing her heavy earrings, which pulled down through the lobes' flesh—as I might have touched with my tongue, as a child, the space a loose tooth left when it fell out.

I remembered the times in college when we'd come back to her room after parties and I'd sit on her bed and wait for her to take off her jewelry so that we could talk. These moments always broke my heart because she did it so slowly, never talking: glittering earring then glittering earring; next her multiple bracelets in one thick bangle; lastly the shiny catch that held together her flyaway hair—all of it done as if this were a guise that had failed and was now useless.

She'd look at herself in the mirror, unadorned, as if there were one more thing she could take off, like a porcelain mask held upon a wooden stick that she could lower: the mask of her fragile beauty itself. It never worked for her, that particular mask, and after a time I think she failed to see the purpose of it.

IN BED THAT night Aaron reached for me. I could tell he wanted sex badly. And I knew it was Sarah who had aroused him. This was not about me. But I gave in and compliantly lay beneath him, indifferent.

A week more of this, I thought. That's all. Then the bar. And I can break up with him. Why even tell him about Paul? He doesn't love me, he doesn't need to know, he'll only be jealous, it will make him crazy, make him take longer to get over the breakup. It was the pattern of thought I kept repeating, but it never really persuaded me. I knew that everyone, finally, wants to know the truth.

Aaron pushed up my T-shirt. It stayed in a roll just above my breasts. The level of exposure felt oddly medical, as if, in a doctor's office, I were exposing only as much as was necessary, only what pained me. Then he started to pull my pajama bottoms off. I had the impulse to fight him, as if my swatch of pubic hair were suddenly an embarrassment, an obscenity. But I stilled myself.

For a month I had been so detached, so cold to him during sex. I'd felt Aaron's frustration. For a while he'd been especially sweet to me—he'd sent me flowers at the office, insisted we see each other more often. It had seemed a rule with him: the more I ignored him, the more overtures he made. But it couldn't last forever. Now, all at once, I felt him give up.

He pushed my shoulders downward, indicating that I should go down on him, and I complied. He made sure my face was obscured by the wash of my long hair; before, he'd always met my eyes. I had once loved seeing his pleasure; loved, also, the power of giving it. Now it was as if he wanted his pleasure, this time, to be private, as if he didn't trust me or like me enough to let me watch him. And it seemed as if he wanted our sex to transform into something different without his having to ask me for anything aloud. Soon I tasted a watery bead of his semen, salty on my tongue, viscous but nevertheless tasting like the more liquid fluid of my own tears.

He flicked the lights off. It was unlike him. Then he bent me over at the waist so I was on all fours. He arranged my body as if it were immensely flexible and stripped of will, like a department-store mannequin's, its limbs rotating without resistance.

"Yes," Aaron kept saying, "oh yes," as if recognizing that this was what he had wanted all along. He made low sounds deep in his throat. Once I had to cry out because he thrust into me so hard that it was painful.

I wished that I could be somewhere else during this sex while my body suffered it. I knew I wasn't ready to leave Aaron yet. This seemed to be the price I'd pay for staying. He somehow knew to punish me even before he knew, consciously, what I'd done.

MY DESK WAS crowded with piles of photocopied cases. It occurred to me that I could call to have any number of things delivered to me: more photocopied opinions, legal treatises from the firm's library, an expensive dinner. Rather than walk up a single flight of stairs, I could call to have a memo I'd written delivered by messenger to a partner's office on the floor above. The firm allowed me to sit in my office and become simply a mind, thinking. At the moment, though, there was nothing I wanted, nothing this firm could do for me.

I'd been working for several hours when the phone rang. I picked it up, cradling the phone in the crook of my neck.

"Hello?" I said, still glancing at the computer screen and tapping on the keyboard, twisting my mouth to the side in displeasure as I looked at the beginnings of a legal memorandum to a partner. I couldn't get the argument I was making to work; maybe it was wrong.

"Julie?" It was Aaron.

"Yes."

"Stop fucking typing," he commanded me. "You lied to me for all this time. It must have been at least a month, right? Answer me. You bitch. How could you lie to me for all that time? You're an unbelievable schemer. I know you're seeing Arias. I know you saw him last night. You saw him at eight at his apartment, when you said you were at the library. Don't deny it. I'm onto you. I hear he has a serious girlfriend. You two are really charming, you know that? Does he live with her, too? Where the fuck does she think he is all the time? Is she as stupid as I am?"

He paused. I didn't reply.

"Some of your friends don't really like you, you know," he said. "They disapprove of you. They just don't tell you, Julie.

"Don't you have anything to say?" he asked me.

"No," I breathed. I imagined Aaron's eyes gone to disks, dark and wholly reflective like insects' eyes. I couldn't think what to say; I was too afraid.

"All right, then," he said. "If you won't talk, I'll make you listen. You're not going to like what you hear, either. Did you think I liked sleeping with you? Your breasts sag," he said. "You have a fat stomach. I had to bring myself to do it. Did you ever wonder why we didn't sleep together that much?

"You have stretch marks," he added, "as if you were pregnant."

I had wondered whether these flaws would be noticed—the stretch marks from losing and gaining weight, their branchings like fractures in ice. Now I was strangely fascinated, listening.

"You must think I'm an idiot for not catching on," Aaron said. "I thought you were distracted because of your mother. Sarah said that. I felt so *sorry* for you. What a joke. You were fucking some guy and actually you couldn't give a shit about your mother."

"You're right," I said. "You're right about everything."

"That's all you have to say?"

"I'm sorry."

"You're sorry? You know, you think you've ruined my life, but you just wasted my time. I'm going home at eight and I expect you there pronto. Then I want you out."

"I'll be there."

I hung up then, quietly clicking the receiver into its black berth. Then I crossed my arms, as if I were cold, feeling hyperconscious of my body.

I realized there was only one way Aaron could know about Paul: from Sarah, the only person I'd told about seeing him the previous night. Of course. That had been the point of his remark about my friends disapproving. Certainly Aaron had begun something when he held her above the ground outside that Caribbean bar. Something sexual had crystallized in that

tension, in his catalytic touch. He must have called her later—
I'm sure he had his suspicions about me—and badgered her
into telling him.

I had a crazy, momentary feeling that I wanted to complain *to Sarah* about what Sarah had done to me, as if she
were a third person. Of everyone I knew, she had always best
understood how I felt. There were many times in college when
she'd practically discerned my unspoken thoughts verbatim.
Throughout the long course of our friendship, like sisters,
we'd developed an intimacy, an interdependence. When had it
become a competition? The money I made, Sarah's intellectu-
alism; Sarah's thinness, my stamina at school and at work; my
cheating on Aaron, Sarah alone for so long. Now the closeness
that had been comforting seemed dangerous, as if some torque
of anger had torn our intimacy apart and opened up the possibility of our using knowledge against each other. From my
stories about Aaron, Sarah knew him eerily well, better than
he'd think she would. She knew exactly what appealed to him.

I should be angry at her, I knew. But I ached now for any
restraint, even if it was my own: for someone to hold back. I
thought I might forgive Sarah's betrayal just to know there
was forgiveness in the world. I wanted to know that, to be
able to draw from it. And there was a sense in which I wasn't
really capable of anger, ever. If I tried to turn my anger outward, it struck inward instead, burrowing into me. Anger always, inevitably, became sadness for me. I was like a machine

that, overheating, is programmed to shut down into its own darkness, its lights flickering crazily and then deadening with finality.

I resolved not to think about this anymore. For the rest of the day, I attended to the legal documents on my desk, which had their own logic and demands. They set out a neat, implicit agenda for my time, which I billed in fifteen-minute increments to the large corporations that were the firm's clients. I concentrated as hard as I could, willing myself into a trance.

I had only rarely left the firm before nine or ten at night since I'd begun working there at the beginning of the summer. Forced to leave early that day, I felt oddly free. I left the firm's offices stealthily, successfully avoiding being seen by any partners I knew; dashed out through the lobby; and scuttled across expansive Park Avenue, halting on the useless island that divides it. The whirl of people filtered around me, in and out of the buildings and through the skeleton of the gridded streets. I was about to hail a taxi, but I stopped for a moment.

The late-summer sunset caught me out, caught me unawares. It seemed precious, rationed, there at the very end of a cross-street, at the end of the corridor the buildings made. I wished for a second that I could clear the buildings away to see the whole sky. Even then, I knew, this sky, with its grudging yield of color, would not be the sky of my childhood, the sky I longed for—the open, star-filled sky of the tropics, overhead a flawless dark blue that had lightened evenly toward the ground, as if the sun's light barely crept toward me, straining around the curve of the world. Still, I stood there in order to watch the last few moments of the limited New York sunset, to drain the last drop of what beauty was there. Then, when the sky had darkened with finality, I hailed a taxi, because I was being called home.

When the cab dropped me off in front of the loft, I felt some fear, but I also felt very strongly that anything, any particular thing, could be ripped out of me now and I would still live. I would outlive this, too. I had outlived it all so far. The resiliency of my childhood came to me in a rush: both the dread and the knowledge that I would survive.

I think I almost expected an ambush when I walked in, perhaps by both Aaron and Sarah, expected to walk into a darkened room and have a light flicked on by an unseen hand to reveal them both watching me quietly from armchairs, in judgment. Instead, I opened the door to see Aaron there alone.

"Heeey," he said softly, his usual greeting but drawn out in sarcasm to become a longer sound. "Julie." Despite the sarcasm, he looked unsettled, vulnerable, like someone roused from bed in an emergency. His face was dead white.

"Aaron, I'm sorry," I said. Apology was nothing more than a feint to prevent him from striking me. It was my way of cowering.

"Look, I want to settle this quickly," he said. "Get out this weekend, okay? I need to use this place while I'm studying for the bar. Then I'll get out. I'll stay with a friend for a few days, I'll take my flight. We won't have to see each other again. Is that a deal?"

"I have to find someplace to stay." I was thinking aloud.

"I'm sure you have someplace to stay, Julie," he leered. "You know I'm not asking that much, don't you? I just need someplace to sleep for a while, until I take the bar. You have to know how hard I've worked. I'm not taking it again. No way. I am passing it *this* time. Try not to be a total bitch, why don't you."

I nodded. Besides the expansive arrogance, I heard in his voice a touch of the pleading that comes from exhaustion.

"That's fine," I said. "I know you talked to Sarah. Why did you call her?"

Aaron shrugged. "She called me. She told me the truth. I respect that. She doesn't have to lie for you, you know."

He paused.

"Before you leave, Julie, tell me one thing. Did Arias give you the miracle bang, or what? Because it's clear to me that you're not reacting to this at all. You are in outer space."

I just gave him a look and said nothing. I didn't feel anything, I realized; he was right. I turned away from him to go to our bedroom and pack my things.

As I turned, he held on to my blouse and the thin silk ripped loudly along a seam. I couldn't tell if he wanted to strike or to hold me. Two of the buttons gave at the same time and skittered in clicks of plastic across the floor.

"I'm sorry," he said, bending to pick up the buttons. "I know that was expensive. I didn't mean that."

He offered me the two small, shiny buttons. I took them from him and then let them fall to the floor again.

He raised his hand as if to hit me, but he did not.

I was lucky. He had it in him to do it. In a flash I recalled a time when, drunk and frustrated, he'd punched the wall of a beach house that a group of law students had rented during the winter. The thin white wall simply broke nicely into a hole a little larger than his fist, like a break in snow with a crust of ice.

I fled to our shared bedroom. I switched my ruined blouse for a sweater in a moment, performing the whole motion as quickly, and with as little exposure, as a junior high school girl changing in a locker room. I looked behind me several times as I packed my suits for work. Then I slipped out.

I was sleepwalking through all this in shock, my body performing its motions, my mind in some reverie of its own. All that was left to me was thought, and a certain sexual impulsiveness. As for sadnesses, I could not fully feel them, but could only register them in some analytic and intellectual way, store them somewhere so that someday they could be felt.

My extreme detachment during this time reminds me of the beginning of a short story I read in a college class; it was used as an example of mixed "person." I remember the first sentence: "The girl (myself) is walking through Branden's, that excellent store." I felt as if I were watching "the girl"—who was strong, ambitious, rational, who I knew would negotiate this thing, would live beyond this time. Only dimly, parenthetically, did I realize that the girl was also myself and fear what might happen to me, what this time would do.

SARAH AND AARON were gone from my life, cut out of it as if by a single stroke or blow. Now a single intimacy remained to me, the peculiarly limited intimacy, mostly physical, that I felt with Paul. I called him from a street phone, my suitcase on the sidewalk next to me.

"Aaron found out about us," I said without prelude.

"Jesus," he said, and paused. "Oh no."

It was hard to hear him, a phone call like a conch shell, a bad connection but I didn't want to break it.

It was the first time I'd heard his voice less than utterly confident. I could tell he was working out the import for himself of what I'd said. Aaron knew who he was. Now Angela might find out that he was seeing me, the firm might. He envisioned the crutched-up structures of our dishonest lives collapsing in parallel, at the same time.

I told him my arrangement with Aaron: I'd leave for the weekend, then I'd have the loft afterward, although Aaron could come by to pick up his things before he left for Barcelona.

"Why are you doing that?" he asked. "Don't run that kind of risk when you don't have to."

It was as if he had some special access to Aaron's anger, though they'd never met.

"Just go to a hotel," he suggested instead. "Hotel Chelsea, maybe. It's near your house. Or keep staying with friends. Don't tell Aaron where you are. You and Aaron are rich New York lawyers, not some divorced Russian couple forced to live together because they can't find a new apartment."

"Of course. You're right," I said.

"Can I see you?" I asked. I heard myself pleading in a slight, grinding mosquito whine.

"Not right now. I'm chained to my desk. Rischoff is really riding me. Talk to you. Bye."

"Bye," I said to the dial tone. Paul often cut off our calls when it suited him, as if he could demarcate my precise place in his life that way.

I couldn't bear the conversation. I could tell he'd wished I'd kept this to myself, as if this crisis were some strategy of mine to force intimacy. He'd backed away from it. It was more unbargained-for feeling. I was only an affair to him. Yet I had wanted more from him than practical advice and the addresses of hotels. I was waiting for some conclusion about what was happening with us—an interpretation, not just tactics. I was waiting, forlornly, to be asked to stay with him. And, of course, I was waiting, in a way, for love.

Annoyed, I thought of calling Angela. I thought of how quickly he'd hung up, without ensuring that I was all right. And I began to conjure up past slights, small resentments—

and pity for Angela, who, I thought, waited futilely to marry him. I decided I could even feel slightly morally superior to him if I called. The difference between Paul and me, I mused, was that I'd been chafing to leave, planning my escape from Aaron, whereas he seemed content to cheat on Angela indefinitely—a careful planner and a weigher of cost against benefit, dispassionate and at some level unknowable.

I decided not to call Angela. Even as I considered it, I knew I could never go through with it. Whatever Paul was, he was also what I'd chosen for myself, what I couldn't leave. And I couldn't betray him. I felt the pull of loyalty at my heart with a sort of relief: I had this small fidelity at least.

I stayed with friends for the weekend and came back to the loft just after Aaron had taken the bar, as we had agreed I could. In exile from the bed I'd shared with him, I chose the loft's spare back bedroom. Belonging to the owners' child, it was the most private room in the loft, the only one with floor-to-ceiling walls. It had one huge window, crosshatched with ironwork.

In the bedroom, a poster was tacked up at the height of a child's eyes—thigh-high to me. It showed a magnifying glass positioned over a butterfly's yellow wing, enlarging its black spots and the tiny veins running through it. In the corner, there was an automatic rocker. I adjusted it to its highest point and set it rocking, clicking down through a set of notches on its aluminum stand, gently falling until it reached the last notch.

I hung up my suit, matching a skirt to a blouse on a two-tiered hanger to make an eerie scarecrow of myself. I draped my stockings over the back of a small wooden chair, where they hung like flat shadows of legs and feet. Then I lowered myself slowly onto the palletlike futon and clicked off the light. I straightened out my body manually, as if it were an object, pressing my palms on my hipbones momentarily. I tried to forget the space and darkness of the rest of the huge loft.

MY EYES OPENED abruptly and I cried out. On his knees, Aaron bent over me, shaking me awake, starting my heart beating fast. I tensed in a second: my eyelids slipped backward, my eyes focused, the corners of my mouth tightened. There was a rush of the scent of alcohol. Aaron's face was distorted by closeness, as if I were seeing him through a fish-eye lens. He was holding down my shoulders. I couldn't move; I felt as if I'd awakened bound.

"Goddamnit. Goddamn you. Do you have any idea what you did?" He was very drunk, out of control, slurring his words.

"I thought about you and Arias during the bar," he said. "I might have failed it."

I didn't believe him, but I felt a certain, limited pity for him. On a day when he'd otherwise be swaggering over having finished the bar, he had to slink instead: cuckolded, his possession stolen.

"I tried so hard for this, to make it work with you. I have worked hard for it, damn it. I spent all that time with you in school, when you were depressed and I wanted to work. Why this guy? What does he have?"

I strained to rise, but he kept holding me down. He started unbuttoning his jeans with one hand and then wriggled free of them, using his feet to pull them down. Then he clambered onto me fully, so heavy on me. He began to run his fingers down the curves of my sides. I tried to shift my body to the side, so I could slip out from under him. He countered by placing his hips squarely on mine, balancing there on the nubs of my hipbones. I could feel his erection.

I put one arm over my eyes as if to block a bright light, though the room was dark. For a second I imagined Sarah, small and terribly light, holding me down with Aaron's strength: her pendulous breasts, her sinewy, skinny arms.

Carefully, Aaron moved my arm away from my eyes. Holding my wrists, he extended both my arms out to the side unnaturally far, exposing the undersides of my elbows, as if he were unfolding a bird or bat's full wingspan, spreading the wings into a position they'd never naturally take except in flight, leaving the small warm mammal's body writhing in the center. Then he thrust hard, pushing his penis, both soft and hard, up against me, pantomiming sex.

"Come on, Julie," he commanded urgently. "Let me fuck you. You let Arias, why not me? What's wrong with me?

"I loved you," he answered his own question dolefully. "That's what was wrong, wasn't it. I loved you so much. You didn't understand."

"Aaron, no," I said. "I don't deserve this."

"You deserve more," he said.

"Talk to me. Let's talk," I coughed out. I was breathless and dizzy. "Maybe I can explain. I didn't mean it ever to be like this."

My voice broke as I said this. I couldn't tell him the truth, that what had ended my innocence, what had corrupted me, was not cheating on him with Paul but abandoning my mother. To have had so hard a test so early in life and to have failed it so utterly—after that, anything was possible. That was when I became bad, the bad daughter my mother was so unlucky to have. Now there was only the lesser question, how bad was I? What could cheating matter compared to that? I thought: What did it matter? I had never fully felt the wrongness of this cheating, never since the first time.

Saying any of this, I knew, would only anger Aaron more. This odd, implausible explanation could make sense only to me. And it was the only thing that made sense to me, in this.

He started moving on me again. I could feel my heart beating. I couldn't stand the thought of having him inside me, of opening again to him. I had never wanted to open to him at all, I realized. I had never trusted him that much. But now I had no choice. I was changing into a sexual opportunity: a woman without significance to him, here in his apartment, un-clothed on a bed. He could do anything he wanted to me. If I screamed in the cavernous loft, no one would hear me from the street. That was what we had liked when we'd rented it. It swallowed sound in its depths. It was private.

The moment passed. Aaron shifted his weight off me a lit-tle, stopped thrusting at me. I think he did not rape me pre-cisely because of how expensive his suits were, how much money he knew he'd make. Perhaps he reflected that he would get everything else in life he wanted if he could simply get past this.

"You let me do this to you all the time," he said. "You just lay there. Did you even like it?"

I didn't answer, only breathed full breaths. I suddenly felt safe, as if he had been a person inside the costume of a movie monster whose brown eyes had suddenly become visible through the eyeholes of the pasteboard mask.

"I fucked Sarah after you left," he said. "In our bed. I loved it," he said defensively. "It was great. She has a fantastic body. Not like yours. She's so beautiful. It was great.

"It was so great," he said, a last time. And then he started to cry.

He moved off the futon to sit on the throw rug next to me, still with an erection, shaking.

"Oh God," I said. "Oh Aaron."

I had never seen him cry before. He was not the type to cry.

In the partial darkness, I saw his face wrinkle and contort. On the ceiling above him was a sprinkling of glow-in-the-dark stars colored a pale, fluorescent green: the promise of a sky, from the owners to their child.

"You're so far away," he said. "I was . . . I thought . . . For months you've been so far away. What would it take to get through to you?"

He rose.

"If I can't trust"—he slurred it into *trusht*—"anyone after this, it'll be your fault. You made me this. All the worst things in me, you brought out."

I nodded groggily.

"You made me this," he repeated.

He walked over and opened the door of the child's room, a tall shadow in the doorway casting a sheet of bright light onto the carpet.

"I don't want to see you again. If you come out of this room, I'm just not responsible," he said. Then he shut the door.

I didn't move for a while. He hadn't actually hurt me, but I felt broken. I felt as if it would be difficult to move, but knew that I could. Soon I rose and checked to see whether the door locked. The button at the silvery knob's center kept popping out. Despite this, I eventually slept again, the sheets twisted around my legs, a slight flush warm on my skin like a fever.

In the morning, I realized it was the day Aaron was scheduled to leave for Barcelona; he'd arranged to leave just after the bar exam, I remembered. I left my room and stood quietly in the center of the loft, listening, until I was assured that he was gone.

I wondered later: Could I have told him, all along, about my mother? Had he really loved me all along, as he had said? And if he had, was that why he had threatened me in the end, out of his great bitterness? It was possible that there was more there than I had seen, than I was able to see. In not letting him know me, I had failed to know him as well. Without that, all we had together was a series of nice dinners, conversations about classes and law firms, a beautiful loft.

Aaron had good reason to hate me, I thought: there had never been anything at stake for me with him. What I held back from him was much more than what I ever told him. He had never inspired enough trust for me to tell him about my mother's dying and without that all the other possibilities for us had seemed to me to drop away. Yet maybe I could have told him; he'd learned something about it from Sarah, anyway. Because I hadn't told him about my mother, I could never care enough about him or, later, care enough about cheating on him. I wondered if everything always came down to her; if it always would, for me.

My long flight from my mother and her dying had taken me past the borders of some warm, well-lit place, like a small American town, into its shadowy outskirts. I had not found a place to rest after this flight. I had been left somehow outside the groups of my friends and colleagues, far outside my relationships with men, with Aaron especially and most of all. Escape was hardwired into me from childhood, so much so that I wondered about my capacity for true fidelity to anyone. I tried to imagine that place of lighted safety I had overshot in eager flight. I wondered whether it was a real place or a place in myself. And I wondered whether there was any hope of my someday returning.

I FINALLY REACHED Sarah on the phone a few days later.

"Why did you tell Aaron?" I asked her.

"I think you have a problem with lying," she said. "You slept with Daniel in college, I just found out."

"After you broke up," I pointed out.

"I asked you about it," she said. "You lied right to my face."

"I'm sorry," I said. "I thought it would only hurt you to tell the truth. It was so . . . over."

"You made such a fool of Aaron," Sarah went on. "I felt sorry for him. But I know I shouldn't have told him. I went over and over it in therapy, asking myself why."

"Uh-huh," I said. I knew it was a form of apology.

"You were in your own world," she continued. "Maybe I thought you needed a jolt. Anyway, I didn't really think about what would happen at the time. He wanted an answer. He is a threatening person, you know."

"I know," I said.

"Did you sleep with him?" I asked.

I knew both of us wanted everything to come out now, for the whole situation to play itself out. And I was curious, because I thought Aaron had somehow gotten through to her, even as other men left her cold, that he was for her what Paul was for me: the one who reached her—maybe briefly, but he had.

"Yes," she said. "He came over to my apartment. You were right, he was so big it hurt me." She paused. "I haven't seen him since. He did call me. I didn't want to see him."

Years later, I ran into Sarah on the street in New York City and we had a second conversation, in a café, about what had happened. The atmosphere was eager. We had already been through the hostile conversation. This was, maybe, the hopeful one. We both apologized again.

She called me afterward and I started to hope that maybe her lapse and mine canceled each other, that the score was evened. That what she'd wanted most deeply, in telling Aaron and in sleeping with him, was evenness. Maybe she'd somehow needed to hurt me—to have revenge on me for sleeping with Daniel, to bring me down from the arrogance of my covert affair with Paul—in order to continue on as my friend. If that was the bargain, I could accept it. Still, our renewed contact was only sporadic and finally it tapered off. At the end, I called her and she never returned my calls. I was both sad and relieved. It was just too strange, I think, to go shopping, to have coffee, as if nothing had happened. We were not really even; we were only both hurt.

I'D ALWAYS FEARED that once Aaron was out of my life decisively, Paul wouldn't want to see me anymore. He didn't call for about a week. Each day my heart sank when I came home to an answering machine whose light remained the deadened red of a cherry cough drop. Ultimately he did call. I should have been annoyed at him for not calling earlier, and for not asking me to stay with him, but I was excited instead. Knowing Aaron had left, Paul asked if he could come to see me at the loft. I thought of how I had once stopped him from entering it, that first night when Aaron was asleep upstairs; how he had prevailed, in the end.

It was Saturday afternoon. A thick stream of light in which dust motes slowly drifted projected down through the loft's skylight. I shrugged into a swingy burgundy dress with an Empire waist. I bent over to spray perfume into the fall of my hair and I rubbed lotion into my legs and arms so that the scent rose from my warm skin. For the first time in so long I felt fully alive, as if I caged a lantern.

He kissed me at the door—a peck, unlike him—and for a moment I thought, We could live together. I kept expecting what I felt for Paul to fade, but it never did. It renewed itself, like the magic jar of silver coins in the fairy tale that, when you reach into it, is always full.

I thought this visit might mean that we had a chance together: it was a sideways hope, one I didn't dare have directly. I'd become so good at barring myself from things, ensuring their impossibility so I could safely imagine them without pain. Now imagination brought risk with it. Still, I couldn't resist. I thought about how we might have a life together, how we might have begun. Tonight we could make love here; tomorrow we would awaken together for brunch, spend the day in the city.

Paul exulted at the loft, its excess of space. He walked around to survey this foreign territory that he now could enter, pacing it as if marking it off. He touched the leaves of the hanging spider plants with their small, new shoots like shooting stars. He ran his fingers through hanging wind chimes—stylized metal doves that made a clear, pure sound when their wings clinked together.

I almost shook, keyed up and eager, clasping my hands behind my back, working to still myself.

"This is such a great place," he said. "Wasted on Aaron, of course." He paused.

"Julie, um, don't . . . I can't see you anymore," he said in a rush. "Things are getting better with Angie," he added.

I leaned hard against the kitchen counter.

"I used to think you'd seduced me for life," he said solemnly, almost shyly. "The pull was that strong. But I think I have to go on from this. I mean it this time. It's not anything you did. I used to blame you for seducing me, but I finally realized it was my own choice."

"I would love to go out with you," I said quietly.

"This is an affair, not a relationship, right?" he said. "I just can't see us doing things with our friends now like a normal boyfriend and girlfriend. We're past that point. We're like friends who know each other too well to go out."

"You don't know me that well," I cautioned him. But I knew he was right. We couldn't go back. We each had listened to the other blithely lie, over the phone, to others whom we were supposed to love. Lying was the relationship's core flaw—like a deep and incorrigible birthmark, replicated on each layer of skin. There was no trust in us, and no candor.

He held me then. I could feel that he was already hard. I stroked my fingers up the thin line at the center of his erection. He took my hand and lowered it to my side. Then he lifted me easily into his arms, tucking in the flaring skirt of my dress, and carried me into the bedroom, hefting me as if he were a young groom.

"I do know you," he said as he set me down on the bed.

"Maybe," I said, unconvinced.

He was looking straight at me and my face broke under his scrutiny.

"You put me through the whole gamut, you know," I told him.

He uptilted my face with his hand, as if I were a child, and gave me an inquiring look.

"Yes," I said impatiently. "I know you're leaving. I know this is the last time. This is still what I want."

"You're a beautiful girl," he said. "You should have a real boyfriend."

I shrugged.

He undressed slowly. I thought about how well his simple, striking good looks—appealingly un-middle-American, with a touch of downtown—had done (and would always do) for him in life. About how I had to scratch my way upward to be with him, with considerable and constant effort: always over-dressed next to him and fully made up, eyebrows carefully plucked and lips outlined and then filled in with a lighter pink. I knew I looked pretty sometimes, but it seemed a construct, a careful cosmetic overlay. His handsomeness, in contrast, seemed to be a reality that resisted obscuring, transcending his careless clothing. His face was so beautiful sometimes that it could not help but make me sad. I could see how effortless life would always be for him, how little he could potentially care about it—how aimless his smile, turned outward to the world, could sometimes be.

After Paul finished undressing, he sat behind me to stroke my breasts. I felt so grateful that he loved my body, as Aaron had hated it finally, that he accepted the softness of my breasts and my belly's convexity.

He entered me when I was not yet ready. It was a little painful. I held him off for a moment to adjust to it, keeping him half entered inside me. Then I let him continue. Soon his pace quickened and what I felt from him sexually was release, abandon, epilogue: a certain wildness of acting without consequence, as if the present were already somehow safely part of the past.

After a while I indicated that I wanted to switch positions. I wanted suddenly to be above him, to master my own desire, to release it, bring it to a conclusion, and have respite from it. I started to move to be on to of him, but he fought my motion, trying to finish himself. Arousal slackened and loosened his mouth a bit, making him look a little stupid. I saw aggression in him. I'd known before that he didn't care particularly about my pleasure, but I hadn't thought he would fight against it.

I think he fought me then in some degree of desperation, not out of sheer cruelty: out of his deep wish to defeat my steady gaze—that gaze that had known him better day by day, inexorably; that he knew had judged him. He needed to preserve our sex as the process of his appraisal, his arousal, and his release.

Determined, I fought his thrusts more, moving to break his rhythm. He let me move to be on top. Then he slowed down enough so that sex was erotic for me, building subtly, but so that it was a little too slow for his own pleasure. He knew he must let me come.

I shivered with the orgasm, when it came, my head going from side to side slightly, as if I were a horse balking, as if I were denying it—or as if, just as I was feeling this sharpest pleasure, I were also shuddering at the loss of him.

He came a moment later, easily and quickly, and then we lay beside each other on the bed I had shared with Aaron so unhappily for so long.

Paul had seen that I'd teared up, coming, and he asked me what was wrong. I said it was nothing. We lay as close together as college lovers—sweet late-adolescents sleeping in a narrow monastic bed. But he did not hold me. He turned his back to me, and I turned my back in response, his smaller double. Our bare backs reluctantly touched, skimming each other's skin. I knew that in several hours he would leave me.

He left before the morning, dressing in darkness, easing the loft's door closed. I craned my neck to catch a last glimpse of him, but I saw only the door—the half wall, really—displaced and then continuous, as if there had never been an opening in it. Only with the click of the door did I realize all that I felt. I knew it with certainty and in fullness only in losing him. I loved him, or he was the closest I came. After this, my love for him—like my grief for my mother—would have to stay in the deep back of my mind, where I could neither fully feel it, nor ever crush it out.

Chapter Five

THE SUMMER AFTER I graduated, I lived in the same huge loft again, with three roommates, and worked for another law firm in the city. I heard that Aaron was surprised I was living in the loft, but I wanted, in a way, to show him I wasn't scared to do it. It seemed likely to be an uneventful summer—I would work, then prepare to take the New York bar.

Life was routine, but I was still death-haunted. Though I sometimes thought I evaded it, my mother's slow and prolonged dying always came to reach me. It hung suspended in my life, like the man-o'-wars of my Hawaii childhood—small jellyfish that float in the waves, dripping a clingy blue tail of plasm from a transparent bubble. They would sting me just when I'd forgotten the possibility they might be there.

That spring, my aunt had sent me more nursing home reports about my mother. Fragments of descriptions from them haunted me later, fascinating me and also evoking horror: a mix of fear and revulsion at what the body is and can become. I still could not fully realize emotionally what I knew intellectually: that these reports were not a story, they were about my mother's life.

For a time, my mother vomited every morning, as if she were pregnant. She often had the delusion that someone inside her was trying to strangle her. She tried to wheedle the doctors into removing this other presence inside her; then things would be all right, she said. Sometimes she struck out until she bruised her knuckles and her hands had to be strapped to the bed, but the strikes were purposeless, undirected. From marks on the walls, the nurses could tell that, even alone, she still struck out. Once she grabbed at the crotch of a male orderly. Once she screamed as loud as she could until she was sedated. Once she chewed her own tongue into blood.

I wondered how much longer her life could go on like this. And how much longer mine could as well. I remembered Anne Sexton's line in a poem written after a funeral—"In another country people die"—and thought about the separate country my mother was in and how far away it was.

In later reports, my mother's aggression stopped. Her weight, which had ballooned to almost two hundred pounds in the preceding year, began falling precipitously. Some days she barely moved at all. Her face became impassive. She was stable, in this state, for months.

Later, from another report my aunt sent me, I learned that one day my mother had awakened. Her blue-eyed stare broke. She blinked repeatedly. Her head turned.

The nursing home attendant on duty must have been startled beyond believing it. Sitting by the bed, she made notes for my aunt, knowing time was precious.

The attendant wrote down that my mother said she liked to drive Chevies. That she liked to wear White Shoulders. She said also that her daughter was in college and that she was intelligent. And she said that she thought her illness might have been caused by her divorce. Then she pleaded with the attendant: "Give me a chance. Give me a week."

"I'll give you anything you want," the attendant said quickly. But a moment later my mother returned to her prior, impassive state.

The Chevies. White Shoulders. My starting college. Had these, the last of her memories, been ground so strongly into her mind that they remained when other knowledge was lost, as if they had made grooves, deep neural paths? Or had they hidden themselves in so many different pockets of her mind that at least one reference remained even when large areas of her brain were wiped out, glutted with an excess of fluid that I imagined as drowning the electrical crackles of neurons?

From books, I knew this was the way her illness worked— through a fatal imbalance of brain chemicals, a worsening storm in the brain's chemical weather. A drought of acetylcholine, a flood of beta amyloid. It was odd: after the divorce, her anger had seemed fluid, too—a red liquid infusing thought like blood diffusing in the brain.

She'd asked for so little, I thought—for only a week—in that ghost flicker of electricity in her brain, in the voice of the thought that was dying in her. She could have said, "Cure me." I thought of how little my mother had ever asked for, how little she had ever been given.

And even the mere week she'd wanted was not given to her. She got only a few minutes to try to make herself understood. Her mind had a single moment of clarity, like the moment when a candle is almost exhausted, when the flame flares up just as it dies into liquid wax. Only a stranger was there to hear, to record.

My aunt had enclosed a letter with the report, in which she suggested that, if I visited, my mother might "come back" again. Like the cars and perfume my mother had mentioned, my voice, my presence in the room, were familiar to her. They might bring back a world.

I COULD NOT keep my voice steady when I booked the flight to Tucson. It took so much for me to do it, even this small thing. I wished someone could know how much.

After I booked the flight, I dared to measure the time and calculated that it had been three years since I had seen my mother. "You didn't visit for years," I whispered to myself, as

I would over and over after she died. "You left her alone as she died." I could not speak it aloud, even to myself. It was the unforgivable thing, the worst of my secrets. My choice not to move to Tucson, I knew, could be understood by other people and forgiven. My aunt was there to visit my mother and check on her. For me, moving would have meant interrupting school. I knew no one in Arizona but my aunt and her family, and I did not know them well. There were reasons not to move. But there was no reason, except my irrational fear, not to visit.

Had I been the one to fall sick in some faraway place, I believe my mother would have come to me. She was overborne by life, but not so much that she would not have come, would not have been drawn back to me a little had I needed her to be. She would not have left me to die—as she would have my father had he been the one. As my father had left her. And as I had left her, for so long.

After I told my aunt I would visit, she sent me a new set of nursing home reports in the mail. One of the reports stated that my aunt had tried to disconnect an IV inserted into my mother's arm at a time when she was sick. (Alzheimer's disease made her extra vulnerable to every infection.) The report noted my aunt's plug-pulling in its usual deadpan style, as just another fact to be cataloged.

I didn't say anything to my aunt about it. Like my aunt, I thought my mother ought to be dead. I would have wanted to be dead in her situation, and I thought that had she been more cogent, she would have wanted that as well. But my aunt's boldness shocked me. She'd done this knowing she'd be caught, daring the doctors and attendants to turn her in. I wondered why my aunt had tacitly told me about this: To share the guilt for it? To procure my implicit approval for what she had done?

I never asked; I will never know. It was another dilemma that my aunt took on, that I did not have to face myself. Was it noble or evil to slip the tube out of that insensate arm? Is it noble or evil to refrain, to turn away, safe in your own body?

MY PLANE LANDED in hot sunlight in Tucson in the early evening and a cab took me to my hotel. For hours I lay in bed, curled up in anxiety and self-protection, knees brought up almost to my chest, ducking into myself as if I were turning over and over in outer space, moving in a slow, spinning path.

I tried to prepare myself emotionally in case my mother did recognize me in case she awakened again. It was sad: I couldn't even bring myself to hope, sincerely, that she would awaken and know me so that I could speak to her. There would be such pathos to the scene: my mother, utterly vulnerable, would have no choice but to forgive me for leaving her, on the chance I would help her now. I didn't want that compelled forgiveness.

But what *did* I want from her? Maybe resentment, or even

anger—that would be almost comforting because I'd associ-ated it with her for so long. Perhaps I wanted just the blank-ness I expected. Or perhaps I feared the worst, that she would awaken love for her that was still in me, at that deepest layer I never touched. I had lived on the very surface for so long. I had remained above feeling in life, as if it were a river that moved, turbulent, beneath a scratched windowpane of ice.

I dreamt that night that I visited my mother in her room at the nursing home. She was as my aunt had described her: para-lyzed, her bodily functions frozen, unable to speak or respond. I left the room. When I returned, she was gone, her Velcro re-straints undone, and in her place, sitting on the bed, was a huge, placid beast. It had a dog's floppy ears but a cat's flat, pink nose, nostrils clearly outlined. It lolled on my mother's bed, black-coated, with sharp teeth; its rank smell hung in the air. Its pelt had a glossy sheen, with lounging rolls of fur like a shar-pei's.

It looked at me and said in a deep, dulcet voice, "You're late."

I woke in fear, my heart beating rapidly, my body tense and waiting, as if ready to defend itself. My thoughts were wild, disordered: "I have to go to her," I thought. "I've been letting something kill her. I've been letting her die."

The beast looked different, but I realized it was the same one I'd known in dreams long ago: the animal presence of dis-ease, like that of a predator, choosing. That beast was at the height of its powers now. It had taken on a concrete form, acquiring detail. It had been fleshed out into specificity. It had drawn life from my dying mother.

The next morning, I rose several hours before my aunt was due to arrive. To try to calm myself, I lay by the hotel pool in a black bathing suit, wearing tortoiseshell sunglasses, appearing to be the New Yorker I now hoped I was. My dislike for Arizona was easy and quick. I disdained the artificial-seeming reddish rock formations I could see from the hotel, and the amiable, tan sunbathers with their pastels, visors, and cheap turquoise jewelry.

I smeared sunscreen on my fishbelly-pale legs. The coconut suntan lotion mixed with the sweat on my skin to form a warm film, comforting me slightly. Still, I felt a sort of hopeless dread, an irrational foreboding that I would go to the nursing home and never leave. I realized this had been the fear beneath my fear that by visiting, I would somehow be entrapped: the fear that, like my mother, I would die here; that for me, as for her, youth would offer no protection. I imagined myself sickening and becoming wizened beneath the film of lotion, in the hot Arizona sun.

When it was nearly time for my aunt to arrive, I washed myself off in a standing shower near the pool, pulled on a pair of jeans and a shirt over my bathing suit, and stood waiting near the hotel's circular driveway.

MY AUNT'S LARGE, air-conditioned car had tinted windows, so I couldn't fully make out her face until she stepped out. Her foot touched the curb, her sockless, tan ankle visible above her Ked. Getting out of the low, slung-back driver's seat to greet me, she moved slowly; she had some weight to heft. She rose toward me.

She wore a loose jumpsuit. Her hair was bleached to a light brown, her skin deeply tanned. Her brown-tinted sunglasses, like her blue-tinted car window, were shaded in gradations. She flashed in the sun with gold jewelry, a record of her anniversaries. A plain, heavy woman in her fifties, she looked eerily similar to the way my mother would have looked had she not become ill.

My aunt Betty looked me over carefully, resentfully. I was glad I was wearing old jeans, a cotton shirt, no makeup. Now that I'd finally come to Tucson, far too late, my aunt seemed only half satisfied. It wasn't much of a victory for her.

"I don't know why you picked such an expensive hotel, Julie," she began, her tone barely civil. "This is one of the nicest hotels in Tucson, you know. It's not as if your mother couldn't use that money you make."

"I booked it through the law firm," I told her. "They have a discount."

She drove me to the nursing home. Our conversation in the car was cursory—speech without import to break silence. The nursing home, one story high, was topped with brick-colored tiles. The wings in which the patients' rooms were located fanned out from the central reception desk.

My aunt walked me to my mother's room.

"You need to make sure to clean her up when you feed her," she said to a nurse outside the door. "I found food on her yesterday when I came in."

I took advantage of their conversation to enter the room alone.

The figure of my mother, sitting upright in the bed, was half obscured by a curtain on a runner. I walked around the bed so I could see her.

I don't know how to describe exactly how my mother looked, or if I even want to. If I'd had a child there with me, I would have preserved the child from seeing her. The way she looked was an argument for innocence, for a life lived free of the knowledge of death. It was hard for me to fathom how you could see this and, afterward, just live. The knowledge would beat against your heart to be let in, insistent as the sound of an emergency bell.

To begin, she looked as if she were starving. I knew from the hospital reports that the swallowing response was one of the basic functions her brain had once overseen and now could not fully govern. Precisely those functions of her body she'd assumed all her life—the ones the brain stem regulates automatically—were failing her now. Some nutritive substance, white and milky, flowed into her arm through an IV.

She had always been taller and heavier than I was. Because she spoke loudly, she had seemed to me to be even bigger.

Then the sickness had made her obese. Now she was so thin and small that I could have carried her.

Her whole body was a frozen rictus, a still convulsion. Her mouth was held wide open, rigid as if in horror, as if gasping; her teeth were mossy, yellow and rotting. But every so often her face relaxed slightly and an expression crossed it, seeming half voluntary. I could almost catch, fleetingly, what emotion she felt. It was like watching someone have a particularly visceral memory, or a cat jerk in its sleep. She had experiences, her life went on somewhere, but she was not there, not in the room with me.

The bright, clear light blue of my mother's eyes had not changed—as if the eyes had traveled intact, over time, through different metamorphosing bodies—but the pupils were fixed, unmoving. That stare: I was looking for her in this body, and I had thought I would see her in her eyes, but I did not.

The flesh on her face was baggy, crinkled. It caved in on itself like the skin of a rotten apple, creating vertical runners in her cheeks. I had to remind myself she was in her early fifties. For so much of her life, her disease had been latent—waiting for an invisible, silent clock within her to run out. Then it had begun to show itself in her behavior—her handwriting, her increasingly out-of-control angers. Only in this very last stage had the visible signs of the disease come to her, but they'd done so with a vengeance.

Next to her, on a table, were the restraints with Velcro-covered straps and plastic buckles that I had read about in the reports, left there in case she lashed out.

It was this death-in-life, this halfway state, that my aunt had wanted to extinguish, I realized. My aunt loved my mother —her sister, her opposite, the girl she'd fought with, slept next to, with whom she had grown up—and what she had wanted to kill was not of course my mother, but her death. I envisioned my aunt sitting in the chair I occupied, waiting until the nurse left, pulling the IV out. There would have been blood welling from my mother's arm, bereft of the IV. Yet my mother would not have reacted; she would have done nothing to stanch the blood, would not have cried out at the tug when the IV was withdrawn. Blood would have flowed down her insensate white arm like sap on a tree limb. My aunt would have watched her and waited for the relief to come, waited to see my mother truly at rest. But the nurse would have come in—upset, shocked, businesslike? She would have slipped the IV back in. It was her job. Then the nurse would have made her notations. Did she say anything to my aunt? I could not imagine what.

"Mom?" I said once, timidly, then again more loudly. She did not respond. She'd forgotten me, the images on her retina, the references in her mind, all washed away, washed out.

"Can she hear you?" my aunt asked, still outside the door.

I saw my mother turn slightly, just perceptibly, toward the sound of my aunt's voice.

"No," I said. "I think she hears you, though."

My aunt came into the room. With a flick of her hand, she sent the curtain around my mother's bed skating along until it was bunched at one end of its runner. Then she reached over to carefully shut my mother's mouth, gently pushing it upward with the flat of her palm as if it were a hinged puppet's mouth.

"Patty?" my aunt said loudly. My mother didn't respond.

My aunt motioned toward a set of photographs Scotch-taped to the door of the cabinet next to the bed. "I put those up so the staff remembers she was once a full person, with a life and a family," she said.

The photos were from the old family album Betty had held hostage since she flew out to New Jersey by herself to pack up my mother's few belongings. She had said she would give the album to me if I ever visited Tucson, but now that I had come, I didn't want it. Typically, what I wished most that I could retrieve, though I knew it was impossible, were the books of my childhood. They'd been lost somewhere, left behind in my mother's move here.

My Harvard graduation photo bore the year and my aunt's handwritten note in huge letters: "Julie—Harvard!!!" My aunt must have written it, I realized, when my mother could still, barely, read and see.

"I need to stop in at work," my aunt said. She worked part-time as an actuary, handling pensions. "I'll leave you with her for an hour or so."

She left. I sat down again on the vinyl chair next to my mother's bed. I was sweating, clammy in the bathing suit under my clothes.

After a moment, my mother made a low noise. It was like a small rumble. I wasn't sure if it was a word. In a second, she calmed back down into perfect, rigid stasis.

I looked back at the photos on the cabinet. In one, my mother is in the hospital, pregnant with me. She is very young, full faced and pretty. I'd studied the photo when I was little, thinking of myself there inside her. In the photo, she's managed to sit up in bed, weak with complications but still with her "face" on—with mascara and pink lipstick—smiling. The tray table of her hospital bed holds a box of black licorice bits with tiny, crunchy pink-and-yellow balls of gelatin in their centers, and cardboard jigsaw-puzzle pieces in many different shades of brown. It is the brand of puzzle she liked best, Springbok, with lots of pieces and a cloying poem on the back of the box. When I was very small, we'd finish a puzzle together and then she'd read me the poem.

"I'm sorry, Mom," I began softly. "I should have visited before. I didn't really know what I was doing."

I waited. There was no trace of a response from her. She'd moved in recognition of my aunt's voice, at first, but hearing mine she was still. She'd heard my first word, I thought, and recorded it in a baby book, so many years ago. But now my familiar voice was lost to her. As she was now lost to me.

"I wish it could have been different between us," I said, more loudly now.

Her face stayed precisely the same, her eyes fixed on some point in the distance. She was in another world, as if in a virtual-reality machine, seeing things no one outside saw, making abrupt motions and sounds that were effective only in some other place. When I looked into her eyes, I thought for a moment that I saw terror, but that might have come only from their light, frightening blue. A moment later I saw only blankness.

"I wish it could have been different," I began again. I think I was mumbling. I didn't believe she'd really hear. "I really wanted it to be. All my life, I wanted that. Maybe you did, too. I guess you must have. I don't think your life was fair. I don't think there was any justice in your life, ever."

I felt paltry, stilted in my emotion. I did not say that I loved her. Something was tearing at me, but I thought it could not, after all this time, be that.

I spoke to her for a few more minutes, until I knew my voice could not wake her. She remained still, isolated like Sleeping Beauty within her circle of thorny, impenetrable rosebushes. Except that, of course, she was not the beauty in the fairy tale but its hag, witchy and visibly dying, and she did not sleep, but wavered in a tantalizing limbo between sleep and wakefulness, as if any moment she would awaken. The truth of the comparison was only in the perfect symmetry of her isolation

—the mind cut off within her skull's globe, unreachable—
and in my belief that there was blood on me, deep scratches
rasping, from coming to her.

I began to feel small pains high in my nose and at the corners of my eyes, sharply demarcated and intermittent, like the
sound of ice cracking in warm water. But I couldn't cry, even
though I wanted to. I could feel my eyes become raw and red
and tear up. The inability to cry felt like a failure of nerve. I
had the thought that I would die if I never cried about this, if
I never felt it, that it was too much to hold within me. That I'd
open my wrists someday, if only to free it: her contained death
coming out in blood, violently.

I wanted to shake her, to try to get her attention, to make
her know that at last I had come. To shake her and to say: Are
you alive? Are you awake? Are you a dead person outside a
proper grave? Are you yourself anymore, or another thing?
Were you ever mine? Why are you my mother? I wanted to
scream, too, to shout at her impassive face, but I could not
even try my voice at it. I was passive. What I did well was
complete assignments, take exams, answer questions that
were asked of me. I did not do things in the world. I did not
even drive. And I had not moved to help her. I was no one's
rescuer. And I would not change suddenly into someone ac-
tive and effective like my aunt.

I reached over tentatively to touch my mother's hand. Her
skin felt extremely dry. It was bare; I wondered, for the first

time in my life, what had happened to her wedding ring, whether it had been sold during the divorce, the proceeds split. As I touched her, I pressed down only slightly, because I could not bring myself to caress her. It was awful, but I had always felt with her that with any small concession I could lose everything.

She made no response. I withdrew my hand. When had I last touched her? I wondered. My family had very rarely touched and, when we did, it was always awkwardly.

How had I escaped that body? Why was I allowed to live, apparently intact? Why did she live in her body and I in mine? It had been so many years ago, but it still seemed so miraculous that I'd come away from her whole: from her body at birth and then out of her grip when I'd fled to college. If a woman dies in childbirth, I thought, she becomes only the chrysalis of her child, the papery husk of slick life, slipped off behind it. She may be cancerous, dying. She may die in the act of birth. Life can crawl straight out of death.

So late in my life, I felt a sense of wonder at having survived my childhood. It was as if I'd been battered then and, one day, grown up, a long time since, had touched my bones, surprised to see that they were whole. Because I had felt them shattering.

I swallowed down the salt taste in the back of my throat and I felt the sting of tears that had almost come.

I sat silently with my mother, listening as the heels of

women visitors clicked on the nursing home's tiled floor and the soles of nurses' soft white shoes squeaked as they padded by. After a while, an attendant, a young woman dressed in a white uniform, entered.

"Are you her daughter?" she asked.

I nodded. We introduced ourselves.

"I'm sorry we haven't met before," she said. "Can you just move aside a little so I can get better access to her? She's having more and more trouble swallowing."

I pulled my chair back.

On the bedside table, the attendant set down a Styrofoam tray divided into different compartments. It held food crushed to mush or strained almost to liquid: a grotesque version of a TV dinner. The lumps of food, uniform in texture, were distinguishable only by their color—two browns, one lighter than the other; a pea green; an orange; a yellowy white.

The attendant tipped my mother's chin upward, cradling the back of her neck, and began to spoon food into her mouth. My mother choked most of it back up, blinking rapidly.

I don't want to see this, I thought, but I couldn't muster the strength to stand and leave.

"Do you want to help?" the attendant asked me. "Sometimes the patients respond better if it's a relative. They may seem to be out of it, but they might recognize you on some level."

"No, um, not today," I said.

This was what my mother needed from me now, I realized, this patient process of feeding. In a sense it was all she needed, all that could be done for her. Still, I didn't move to help. I only watched.

My mother swallowed the white substance more easily than the others.

"Still has a sweet tooth," the attendant said. "That doesn't change."

She chuckled.

"Come on," she said to my mother. "Thatta girl."

Being fed, my mother seemed dependent, innocent, like an overgrown child who would grow up only into death. I knew that if I had a child later, feeding the child would recall this scene to me—its messiness and coaxing, the flecks of strained food everywhere, like tiny orange and green pen marks on the attendant's coat. I was almost never around children; I would not recall other children being fed. I would instead remember this.

My aunt returned in the midst of the feeding. The corner of her mouth twitched to suppress a smile of satisfaction. She must have seen my reddened eyes and believed I'd cried. She greeted the attendant familiarly. She sees this every day, I thought. How does she stand it?

"You're lucky not to see them change her," she commented to me.

"Anything happen?" she asked. "She wake up?"

I shook my head.

"That's a shame," she said. "I thought she might."

When the feeding was over, my aunt leaned over my mother.

"Do you want to tell Julie anything?" she asked her. "Do you want to tell her you love her?"

No response.

"Do you want to tell your mother you love her?" she asked me.

"No," I said. "I talked to her before."

"Let's go, then," she said. "Let's get outta here."

We left my mother's room.

I was formal and cold to my aunt, but I admitted to myself privately that however she acted toward me, she was wonderful to my mother, kind far beyond her duty. Recently, she'd transferred her from a bad nursing home with unresponsive attendants to this better, more modern one. I'm sure it was unspeakably awful for her to be driving down the street, my impassive mother in the passenger seat making unintelligible sounds, wondering what she would do if my mother died there.

It was hard for me, dressed in my New York black and with my degrees, to admit that this crude, crass woman was in this respect by far my moral better. Still, in a way, the admission felt as if it cost me nothing. My ethical judgments of myself seemed detached, as if they had no consequences for me anymore. My early life had acted as a blue flame that had burned me down to the pragmatic, surviving minimum—the way a fire on the highway burns a car down to its frame.

There was little else for me to do in Tucson. I met with a hospice volunteer who smoked copiously with my aunt. She obviously disliked me because my aunt did (maybe that was the support the hospice worker gave her). She asked me if I had any questions. I did not.

And I ate dinner with my aunt's family, swallowing mechanically.

"How much do you make?" my thirteen-year-old cousin, a tanned skateboarder, asked me. My aunt's children had picked up their mother's contempt for me.

"Can I ask that?" He turned to his mother.

"Sure," my aunt said.

"Not that much," I said. "I'm still in school. I have a summer job."

"C'mon, how much?" he asked.

"Seth," his mother interrupted. "That's enough."

Halfway through dinner, I went to the bathroom and was violently sick. I couldn't vomit, but I retched and convulsed and my mouth filled with the taste of bile. I looked in the mirror and saw that I had flecks of white spittle on my lips, as if I were rabid, and I wiped them off.

Being in Tucson was panicking me, making me sick, making me breathe shallowly and speak quickly. I had to get out.

I quickly left my aunt's house after dinner, checked out of

my hotel, and took all my things to the airport, where I waited for hours, sitting on my suitcase, and got on the first standby flight to New York I could.

AT THE END of that summer, after I took the bar, I took a few weeks off before beginning a judicial clerkship in Boston. I was the last of my roommates remaining in the loft.

One day in the midst of this vacation, I picked up the phone and heard my aunt's voice.

"Julie?" she said. "It's your Aunt Betty. Your mother died this morning at around ten-thirty. She went very quiet and peaceful."

"Thank you for calling me," I said.

"I've arranged to have her cremated," she said. "As soon as I can leave the kids with someone for a couple of days, I'm going to take her ashes to West Dennis"—the Cape Cod town where she and my mother had grown up—"and go out on a boat some afternoon to scatter them. I think she would have liked that. You can come with me if you want."

"I think I'm going to have to work," I said. Although some part of me longed to go, to touch the ashes that had been her body and then to free myself of them, the part of me that needed to be alone for this, and that did not want redemption, was much stronger.

"Okay," she said. "I'm going to call a few other people. Call me if you need anything."

"I will," I said. "Bye."

I knew I'd never call my aunt back. In fact, I'd never speak to her again in my life, now that I no longer had to.

What I would do now, knowing my mother was dead, was just nothing, I realized. I did not cry. I imagined my aunt on the boat, holding the urn of my mother's ashes, an object that was her possession, like the album of photographs she'd kept. The sea of the off-season Cape would be gray and opaque, so different from the green, translucent Pacific of my childhood, through which reefs could be seen. My aunt would toss away the ashes of my mother's bones, thin as shards of chalk. They would drift on the wind, then descend. For a brief moment, the ashes would float, a confetti on the ocean's surface, rocked by the choppy whitecaps. Then they would sink underwater, until the tiny particles of my mother's body were far separated in the swell of the ocean. After a death, a dissolution. There would be no physical trace of her in the world—in this way it would be as if she had never lived.

I would not know that this was occurring when it occurred. My new job would have started. I'd be in the judge's chambers that afternoon, working, bent over papers, probably drafting a judicial opinion that would transfer money from one corporation to another, and I would not look up. But I would be there with the sift of ashes sinking into the waves somehow, as the ghost watching, as her ghost had all these years watched me.

I SAT AT the kitchen table for a while. Through the gauzy white window curtains, I could see diamond panes of window glass begin to be struck by raindrops. The pattern of light and dark on the table changed with the wind and the force of the rain.

I started water boiling to make tea.

I'm glad she's dead. The thought came to me fully formed, like a telegram. I wanted to disown it, but it was true. I felt a sense of relief. I had always been aware in the deep back of my mind of the running down and grinding down of my mother's mind and body, as if it were a clock's ticking in the room: forgotten momentarily if I concentrated on something else, when I returned to myself it was always there. Now her death was a frozen thing; she did not exist in time anymore. The clock that had governed my life had stopped. I did not live in her time but in my own.

The teakettle gave a high whistle, building up to it through a steam whisper. I found a tea bag to make licorice tea, surprisingly sweet without sugar.

As I hesitated before dialing my father's number, I thought about how he seemed to have a talent for life. The divorce had preceded the start of my mother's symptoms by less than a year, I calculated. Had they stayed together, he would have had more than eight years of unthinkable misery, of catering to my depressed, often furious mother as she became more and more ill. Bearing all this responsibility in such a loveless marriage, he would have suffered an emotional decline parallel to my mother's physical and mental decay. Already reticent, like his Swedish father, he'd have become more and more inward, despairing. What would have been left of him at the end of all those years with her?

Instead, my father was strong. He lived in an alternate time, a parallel world. I knew from our occasional phone calls that in Hawaii he ran and biked and swam in triathlons, the scar on one shoulder from a jellyfish sting shortening the arc of his swimming stroke; he worked on his tan and his musculature, piled his Windsurfers atop his minivan to go to the beach. He bickered good-naturedly with his new wife, drank wine with her, traveled to Europe when he could. They lived together in harmony in the condo she'd ordered perfectly, which I'd visited a few times during college, where opened boxes of cereal were immediately sealed with a plastic clip and there were special graters and knives for every different thing.

My father had had little relationship to my mother's death. My aunt had complained to him about me on the phone; he reported this to me occasionally, without judging me. And once he and his wife had briefly swapped houses with my aunt's family—the swap a product of his guilt, I suspected, because Hawaii for Tucson was not an even trade. Yet in Tucson he had not visited my mother, my aunt had told me.

I dialed his number. After a few rings he picked up the phone.

"Hello?"

"Dad."

"Julie. Did your aunt get ahold of you? She just called me."

"Yes. I know about Mom," I told him.

"Your aunt told me about it, too. Do you know she isn't having a service?" my father asked. "I thought she would, for her kids. But she isn't."

"She didn't say anything about it," I told him.

My father paused. "Julie, there will be some pain for a time, and then it will go away," he said. "Don't give in to it. Just wait it out."

It was the only advice he'd ever given me. Over the years, he had faded out of my life. His acknowledgment of my pain now didn't seem like much. Much earlier, after the divorce, he might have advised me, but not now. I thought about how the pain of my mother's death had gracefully sidestepped him; how at most it had sideswiped him, only grazing him: a near miss. Still, I knew even this spare acknowledgment was emotional for him. Several people in his life, including his younger brother, had died young. He must know this particular pain himself.

Yet he didn't seem to have much more to say to me than this. As usual, he trailed off, leaving silences for me to fill. I have never known how to talk to him. I loved him more than my mother simply because he was decent to me. When I was a child, he didn't assign penalties and rewards or require me to request permission before I did anything. There was no punitive anger in him, waiting to flare. He was reasonable and analytical, willing to explain anything he did, never saying "Because I say so" to close a discussion. But this fairness, it turned out, would only make me respect him; it would never make us close.

"Call me if you need anything," he said finally. "I'm here."

"I'm fine, Dad, I really am," I said. "I'll call you soon, okay?" This was my usual lie. I didn't call often. I would never really call soon.

We said good-bye.

This far and no farther, I thought. This much and no more. For the first time, I was consciously angry at my father.

I remembered the way he'd work on his math research when I was a child, sitting in the corner of the living room sofa, with his brown eyes transformed into big, woeful deer's eyes by the thick magnifying glasses he'd purchased from a drugstore rack. On his lap, he always placed a wooden board he'd made as a backing for his yellow pads and math books, with a nailed-on ledge at the bottom to support his ballpoint pens. The board was covered with doodles of spirals and cubes in various colors, drawn when he paused to play aimlessly in the geometries he knew so well, adding more dimensions, rotating figures to see their symmetries. When he was working, I always yearned to speak to him but feared interrupting. The board created distance in the illusion of nearness. It had been as if the board, and his distraction, presaged his real disappearance. As if, even when he lived with us, his mind was already elsewhere.

When he dies, I thought, he will leave behind a discrete set of mathematical truths, beyond time, unimpeachable, as distant from me as he himself is. My mother had left behind her uncontainable anger and sadness, and myself.

He'd said there would be no service. The formalities, in my family, had fallen away so quickly. My parents' marriage had ended. I'd given up being my mother's daughter. Now, my mother would not even have a funeral. It was all so different from the way it was supposed to be, the way I thought it was in other people's families. I was supposed to go through the trauma of my parents' deaths at roughly the same time my friends did, much later in life. I was supposed to love them and visit them. My parents were supposed to be married, not divorced, so that one could report to me on the other's progress, so that they would be companions in the first death, not alone in it.

It had been different when I was little and my parents were married. I remember wanting to cover a wall with crayon drawings of a cat that had died. I finished ten or so and Scotch-taped them to the wall. It was an effort; we had wanted to make an effort then. I remember that we went to say something over the grave when we buried pets that died, taking the cat and later a rabbit into the hills so that my father could bury them in shoe boxes, turning up the wet soil with a spade. I had put a poem in the shoe box with the small body of the cat.

Now, with my mother's death, the fractured network of my family, what was left of it—severed by divorce and dislike— had failed to keep up even basic decency. Of course, I had failed along with the rest. Make no mistake: I would not have attended a service even if there had been one. I would have stayed hardened to the end. I didn't want to see the Learys, still near-strangers to me. To have to touch them. To recede into myself as they watched. I preferred that they continue to mistake me, distrust me from a distance, that they retain their stark, grotesque image of me as a rich and unfeeling New York lawyer, caring only for money and prestige. My sorrow, if I had any, would be private.

I felt exhausted and the muscles in my shoulders were un- accountably very sore. My mother is dead, I thought again. That meant I no longer had the choice of helping her, nor could I hurt her with my abandonment and feel guilty for it. I wondered again why I hadn't risen to this, to her long illness, why instead of discovering an underground self in me, better than I'd thought, it had only roused a familiar one. I knew with certainty only the impulse to flee, only the way I'd fled from this, the hardest test of me. And I wondered if I would change, over the years, so that someday I'd be able to say I would have done things differently: visited my mother, taken responsibility for her, moved to be near her, forgiven her everything she'd done.

So much time would pass. It was already beginning. I was already living in the time after her death. The years would pass, and her death would get farther away, and therefore smaller, as if seen from a departing train. Finally, it would be like a point, indistinct from other deaths except to me—like a very distant shore recognizable only to the one who calls it home. These years would, at least, serve to dull memory and make my lying easier, so that I could give the excuse of my youth facilely, routinely, and without flinching, even to acquaintances—the excuse that I hadn't been fully grown-up when I'd abandoned her, that I'd act differently now. But I would never fully know this excuse to be the truth. And maybe it never would be. In some way, even if I changed and became a very different person, this would always be mine, this desertion.

LATER THAT DAY, a few of my mother's friends called, including a sweet woman named Lani, short for Leilani, who had been in my mother's therapy group in Hawaii. From my childhood, I remembered my mother telling me (with typically unwelcome candor) that Lani was sexually frigid. And I remembered that Lani was so much younger than my mother that people had mistaken her for my older sister when we all went out together. I remembered Lani braiding my hair and giving me clothes that were too small for her.

"The last time I saw your mother," Lani said, "was after she'd left work and was living alone in that Jersey apartment. I invited her to come to New York for as long as she wanted—I was staying for a week. She chose to come for the whole week."

How lonely my mother must have been, I thought, to choose so rudely. I had stopped visiting by then.

"We went to a play, and she couldn't find me when she came back after she'd gone to the rest room," Lani said. "She was so completely lost. She was so upset." She stopped, thinking.

"I'm so sorry," she said.

"Thank you," I said.

She went on: "I think your aunt was too hard on you. You do what you have to do to survive."

I thanked her again.

Only later did it occur to me that Lani—this person whom I barely knew, who was not even in my family—was the only one who had said she forgave me.

My mother's childhood friend Elayne, who had visited us when I was in high school, also called.

"I was embarrassed to offer your mother help," she confessed. "I felt like Lady Bountiful."

I knew Elayne was happily married and successful in her career, wealthy, with two grown sons who were also successful and who loved her. That must be what she meant, that her own plenty had been an embarrassment that kept her from helping my mother. She thought offering aid would only underscore the dramatic difference between their two lives, which had for a while, through high school, college, and their early marriages, appeared to be equally blessed.

"It's okay," I said to Elayne.

I was no one to judge, that was certain, but I thought about how, when Lani offered the week, my mother had taken it all. And I thought that Elayne should have offered anything, any material help, without a qualm. And that I should have as well. Why had I been so rigid? Why was Elayne so squeamish about the truth her gifts would have acknowledged? There were no philosophical niceties in the horror of this disease; there was no shame in it. There were all the books on tape I had not sent my mother, small amounts of money I could have afforded to give even while I was in school—all the harmless, painless things I had not done. They would have meant something; she would have taken them all. There had been a middle way.

Yet all the Ladies Bountiful whom my mother knew had stayed alone with the bounties of their lives and it had fallen to my homely aunt, who had less, who had little, to give and give and give, as if there were no bottom to her giving, as long as my mother was alive to accept it.

Like Lani, Elayne offered to talk to me about my mother. As with Lani, I turned her down.

My great-aunt Alberta, one of the Learys, called about an hour later. My aunt had told her that my mother had died.

"You seemed like an orphan when you came here from Hawaii with your mother," Alberta said.

I said nothing. I thought how strange it was that she'd said "orphan," as if my mother were already dead then. Alberta had spent so much time with my mother then and it had seemed to me that my mother was most alive when she was with the Learys.

Then she asked me, "Julie, why do you hate your mother so much? Why didn't you ever visit her? Did she abuse you?"

"No, she didn't," I said. I thought: *Not in the sense you mean.* And I thought: *I don't hate her. I couldn't, not after everything that happened.* But I did not say any of this. The explanation would be too long. And I did not feel I owed it to my great-aunt. It was for myself that I would have to work out what had happened to me, and why.

Alberta was silent and got off the phone a moment later. I realized she wanted to forgive me and could not.

I thought of calling John Brunner, but I feared calling this randy, irresponsible man whom my mother had not been able to forget, feared I'd learn more about my mother than I wanted to. I also thought of calling Lani, as she'd offered, to find out what my mother had said in therapy, why she'd left my father and her life in Hawaii. I thought of finally, painfully, talking to my quiet father, of asking him, or my mother's family, for the film of my parents' elaborate Catholic wedding, so that I could for once see her happy—as I never had in life.

As time passed, I didn't do any of these things, as if by remaining ignorant I could protect myself from the full weight of my mother's death.

SEVERAL YEARS LATER, I saw my great-aunt Alberta—then a very old woman, basset-cheeked but thin—on the street in New York City, near Alexander's, her favorite store. She saw me too, and I think she recognized me, and it seemed to me that she set her mouth against me in hate.

I was dressed up for a friend's engagement party, wearing a dress and heels. I tensed to run, but Alberta disappeared into the crowd around me.

I felt oddly sorry: I would have so loved the relief of losing myself in that crowd, of disappearing just as she began shouting at me. I had never been able to do that with my mother, to simply run from anger. It would have been exhilarating to run, in my heels, away from her, so satisfying each time they struck the pavement, so lovely to run, and not to trip, and then to be away.

Chapter Six

IT WAS IN August that my mother died; I cannot remember on what day exactly. In a way, it doesn't matter to me which day my mother, already dysfunctional, happened technically to die. What I really want to know, and never can, is a different date, the date she was lost to the world. A date to be guessed at like the date of a conception, the date some secret, hidden line of communication went dead, static overwhelming it. The end of thought, not the end of breath. The eclipsing end of the last of her memories, like a message on a scrap of paper gradually singed and then in a moment consumed by flame. The end of memory itself. The day she really died.

For a few days after I learned of her death, I closeted myself away, alone in the loft. It was silent, insulated. Sometimes I filled it with music, but more often I did not. Each day the skylight would cast the same pattern of sunlight over the floor. At night the loft got absolutely dark. The glow-in-the-dark stars on the ceiling of the child's room provided the only trace of illumination when I went to sleep, their fluorescence not a real light but the suggestion that light was possible.

I was there alone again, just as I had been during the previous summer after Aaron left. Here I am, I thought with considerable self-pity, a small girl in a flat, small bed in a corner of the only enclosed room in this huge loft, far from its center like a distant planet. There was no one I wanted to call, I realized. Sarah was the only one I'd ever really talked to about my mother. Now Sarah was out of my life. I had shut out family and friends one by one, as if I were closing shuttered windows to a house, blocking out the sift of light through slats to see, finally, what the blue darkness held for me.

I lost weight day by day until a pair of my old, favorite jeans slid off me like a chrysalis. My unwashed hair curled down my back in viny, dirty tangles. I looked at the world from a ghoul's head, eyes bulging in hollows—or so I imagined. Occasionally I would remember to eat and order food to be delivered—small discrete sushi or slippery sesame noodles that tasted like peanut butter. I would answer the door to receive the cartons in dark sunglasses even at night, my head down, mumbling my thank-yous.

Sometimes I tried to read, but I couldn't persist with it, which disappointed me. I'd thought that, as I grew older, I'd have more strategies against loneliness and be able to feel even more satiation in books. But in truth, I realized, books and their consolations had been exhausted for me. I felt addicted to the touch of skin against skin, different from anything else and still not enough. I remembered being in the loft with Paul, that final day the previous summer. He was still in the city. I wanted to call him, but I stopped myself, remembering the aching partialness of seeing him and then having him leave.

I cut myself in the kitchen once during the days I stayed inside and as I held my hand under the tap, I involuntarily sighed at the relief of it. Seeing the blood made me know how unhappy I'd been, how much I'd subconsciously wanted to see blood flowing from my wrists. It made me know how close I was, that I took so much pleasure in the sight of blood.

I thought my accomplishment at this point was that I was still alive, that I had not died of my mother's death. The thought would become ironic, later, when I found out how likely it was that I still might.

I CLOSED UP the child's room, packed my things, and left for Boston. Moving was easy. I had not kept very many things, even selling all but the most essential of my law books. It had been almost as if, for every possession I'd acquired, I'd rid myself of one, to maintain a maximum weight—as if I needed to be able to flee at a moment's notice.

I started work uneventfully, without mentioning to anyone that my mother had died a week earlier. I was embarrassed not to be flying to attend a service and I didn't want to take any time off work to grieve. I hoped that if I were watched by others for a while at work, forced to be "on," I'd be able to stay safely above the full pain that waited for me. Legal work had come to mean solace to me. The myth of myself as an efficient academic machine had consoled me all my life. It had bolstered me, with so little else, for so long.

The judge was brilliant and genteel, the polymath I'd expected. My co-clerks were all nice and smart. My job, to assist the judge with appeals from trial courts' judgments, was safely intellectual. And the judge's chambers—filled floor to ceiling with bookshelves that held volumes of all the published federal cases since the beginning of the Republic—were a sanctuary, divorced from the outside world, as if hermetically sealed: an isolated ivory tower, a house of order in which everything was in its place, where there were no deaths, only wills and trusts.

I wished desperately that I could progress to a place like this court, where loss would be fact and not feeling, where judges could apportion blame and mete out some punishment, or calculate damages and give some recompense. I liked the law's formalization of guilt and expiation. You'd pay, but the damages were in an ascertained amount, and there'd be a time when you would stop paying. You'd be found guilty and a sentence would be imposed, but someday it would end. The law was so careful about fine points of debt and obligation. I had not felt that I could afford such subtlety. I had known only how to flee.

At work, when I was writing analyses of legal issues, I felt as if I could be someone, or something, other than myself. The arguments almost seemed to write themselves, as if they had been structured in advance. There were three-part tests to be applied, state interests to be balanced against individual rights, well-established standards to be cited, and obviously relevant judicial decisions that needed to be either followed or distinguished. What I wrote seemed transparent, without a trace of myself on the page—shot through with the assumption of objectivity and the rhetoric of necessity.

I found the law's completeness very satisfying. Analogies could always be drawn, between disparate areas of law if necessary. The law's seamless web of logic could fill any gaps. The law held for me a compelling promise: that all the world's chaos—its anarchic emotion, its endlessly tangled drama— could suddenly be transformed into order with the stroke of a pen.

Still, the quiet atmosphere of rationality that I enjoyed at work disappeared as soon as I came home each evening. I would often wait all day at work to cry at home at night, as if it were a treat, a reward. I would be racked by sobs and wait for them to pass. Or I would rest my forehead on my stacked fists and sit there suspended in sorrow, my chest tight. I imagined myself as a flesh casing to a pure light blue, lighter than the blue of blood under skin. The blue the sky fades to near the sun, or the blue of a pool filled by wind with rippled white diamonds of light. A blue that wrinkled my interior to bitterness the way swimming turns the pads of fingers and toes to thick raisins.

During the week, I was careful to sleep long enough to erase the traces of crying, so that my face was only a bit pale the next day. On the weekends, I cried inconsolably and my red-lined eyes would ache when I awakened; sleep could not refresh or heal them. My tears always came without any specific provocation, from the long procrastination of a continual grief. Most of the tears, I confess, were for myself, for all the pain this death had brought me. I cried in self-pity. It gave me little relief. Afterward, my chest still felt tight and tense, as if inside me there were an oppressive second rib cage, gelid, smaller than the real one. But some of the tears, finally, were for my mother, and these were the only ones that would free this tightness, as if I were sobbing something out of my body with each breath.

I thought of the time after my mother left her job and moved into Nan's apartment, when she was cogent enough barely to function but had begun dramatically to decline. I wondered if she thought of suicide then—if she even prepared for it stealthily, planning for it like a terrorist there in her New Jersey apartment, in her lost suburban development, largely unnoticed by the world. And I wondered why she did not do

it: if it was a matter of hoping against hope, or simply of letting one day slip into the next, of going to sleep with alcohol
each night until she had neither mind nor will enough to do
it—until she had so little control over the world that she
could turn on the shower and not remember the ordinary way
to stop its water from raining down.

I cried—it was too late—but I cried for the days my
mother spent in her apartment alone with the television, losing her vision. I cried for the long span of time when her mind
was dying into itself like a fruit rotting invisibly beneath its
skin. And I cried for her growing knowledge that her daughter would not come to see her, not in time for it to matter.

DESPITE MY PRETENSE of normalcy, one of my co-clerks, Ben,
soon sensed that all wasn't well. His marriage was ending
then, I later learned. Maybe he knew the more subtle signs of
sorrow from his own experience.

"Is something wrong?" he asked as we were walking home
together. "I know we don't know each other that well. You
just seem a little sad at times. Is everything okay?"

"My mother died a few months ago," I said, exaggerating
the time that had passed. "I'm having trouble dealing with it.
I think it's better if people don't know. But if I burst into tears
someday and have to leave, you could mention it."

"I won't tell anyone," he promised.

His perceptiveness bothered me. I'd wanted to believe I appeared exactly the same as before, just as professional: co-

ordinated skirts and stockings; tortoiseshell sunglasses pushed up on my forehead, an expensive purse, low pumps; a face unlined and untroubled, if a bit pale; bitten nails the product only of garden-variety neuroses.

After Ben's remark, I realized I had no idea how I really looked. All at once I felt like the glass cat in a book from my childhood, as if anyone could look at me and see everything: the brain and its electric flashings; the red heart surrounded by a hanging web of veins. That flinty, faceted heart.

AS MUCH AS I took refuge in the law's abstraction, at the same time it began to unsettle me. The people described in the briefs never entered the appellate court to appear or to testify. Law school, with its artificial hypotheticals, had set me up to accept this detachment, to view a person's life as merely part of an analytical problem to be solved: a paper trail of evidence, a set of facts to be fitted into a web of doctrine, a case with a nickname. But my training hadn't quite taken, I found. I often envisioned the criminal defendants whose appeals I read walking through the courtroom in a long line, manacled together, their heads bowed. I imagined burying my fingers in the spotted fur of a smuggled ocelot pelt that had been intercepted by the government, never making it to the sham reincarnation of taxidermy. I thought about lifting the bricks of cocaine exchanged in the "sting" operations the briefs described—feeling their heft in my hands, watching them crumble at the edges into powder. And I wondered how the real defendants, whom I never saw, fit into the court's paper world of documentation and proof; whether judges could really tailor paper to flesh. It seemed arrogant to think that it was possible to know enough about someone from a paper record alone to affirm or overrule the fate decreed to him.

Had there been photographs included with the briefs, I might have been able to envision the defendants rising, three-dimensional, from the flat page as if they'd been lurking underneath it. But there were no photographs, and I was left to envision them from nothing: their unique faces, their terrible stories as reconstructed in the courtroom, the moment the jury—forever and irrevocably—announced their guilt.

IN EARLY OCTOBER, I received in the mail an envelope that bore my aunt's return address in Tucson. I slipped quickly from the hallway into my small studio apartment in Beacon Hill. Fumbling, I locked the door quickly, as if I were locking it against something, escaping pursuit. I ripped the envelope open, half knowing what I would find, feeling chills. Inside was my mother's autopsy report, dated September 21, 1992. I didn't know why, but for some reason, maybe because of the rareness of my mother's disease, my aunt had paid for this service, the service of turning a body into information. Now the report had come in.

I stood behind the door, reading the report in fascination, in the suspension of real time. It was signed by a Daniel

Wilder, M.D., of St. Francis Hospital in Tucson. I read its clinical recording of the cause of my mother's death: "Alzheimer's Disease—Severe." And I read its detailed description of the final state of my mother's brain, the plaques and tangles of neural fibers that had formed within it. But what broke me in the report, what reached me finally, was this simple sentence: "A few normal neurons remain."

The dispassionate notation of a doctor I did not know, this sentence meant to me that my mother had not been completely crushed out of her body as she was dying, even at the very end: she still thought, still lived. When I'd come to visit her in the nursing home, she was, in some sense, still there. It was still her. Those "few normal neurons" made ghost connections—flickering her thought, in mimicry and half completion, across the scanty lattice of remaining neurons, through decay and paralysis and burned-out memory. Stringy tassels of fiber in her brain still sent small, broken messages in her words. When she'd spoken to the nursing home attendant that once, those few neurons had pulled her back to the world for a moment, as if in the last glare of a supernovaed star, and then she had died back into what she was, and then she had actually died.

I thought of the liquid chemical rising in her brain and the neurons crackling electric. I imagined dendrite and axon, crackle and breakdown, telephone wires in lightning storms fluttering broken, electric eels' green and frazzled zapping under the deepest of dark water, fluid and flood and final insanity. And I tried to imagine how it felt for her to die this way, with the disease in the center of her very self—knowing the disease intimately, powerless to halt it.

The autopsy report also stated simply: "The patient asked her sister for pills to end her life." It was the first I knew of this request. I don't know what my aunt's response was. She may have feared a murder prosecution by the time my mother asked. She may have tried to help my mother, as she had done earlier with the IV.

I wondered why my mother hadn't asked for death sooner. She was the last person in the world to have hope about life. She had been disappointed again and again. Her marriage had ended. Her daughter, she knew, did not love her—not enough to come care for her or visit her. Maybe she hoped anyway, in the irrational way we all do sometimes, in the way that lets us live.

Chapter Seven

———

THE AUTOPSY REPORT seemed, in a way, to close the issue of my mother's death. I thought I might be able to begin a normal life now, and I started to try to have one, going to a few parties on the weekends, seeing friends in the area. For a while, my depression began to alternate with a strange happiness, star-bursting and artificial, that came in crazy swings, my brain chemistry blatantly haywire. I imagined wings sprouting from the backs of my arms: the nubbed beginnings of feathers layered on taut skin, which would grow to graduated lengths, from the shortest pen quills at my wrist to long oar-feathers at my shoulders. I thought of the wings often, of the vault they'd form in flight. I would begin to smile to myself, then suppress the smile. As I did when I was sad, I tried to be alone when I felt this happiness, fearing that others would know it for what it was: false.

Later I began to feel genuinely happier. I often went running along the Charles from Beacon Hill to Harvard, connecting my new life with my old—jogging over a shaky wooden footbridge that resounded with my steps, watching the up-ended ducks near the riverbank, finding the precise perspective on the Hancock Tower that reduced it to a sheer mirror face, with a single notch, that shone with sunset. In the winter, I began to take driving lessons, spun my tires in the snow, spent months being honked at, and finally got my license, passing the easy test Cambridge gave. My co-clerks gave me a small model car to celebrate.

I began dating a friend's friend whom I met at a party, a professional chess player named Nevin who lived in a dive-y apartment in Allston among set-up chess sets, their pieces aligned in neat rows like idle armies. I spent long periods watching him play chess in tournaments, moving pieces with stiff Elizabethan collars over veined marble squares. We spent time with mutual friends, amused ourselves by trying to set them up with each other, had brunch in the same places each weekend, and said we loved each other after a time.

Still, true to pattern, I did not tell Nevin much about my mother's death. And, true to pattern, I was not faithful to him. Paul called me that fall several times to tell me he was visiting Boston to see his parents. I'd known he wanted to resume our affair when I saw him with Angela at a firm dinner dance. As they passed me, he skimmed his hand across the small of my back, his fingers trailing there for a split second, and I caught my breath in a quiet, sharp intake. I knew the touch was about sexual possession, but I didn't look at him, understanding the rules. It shook me. Why is he the one who can reach me, or hurt me, if he chooses? I wondered. Why is he the one who moves me, always?

Each time Paul visited, I cheated on Nevin with him. I did so cavalierly, recklessly, sleeping with Paul a few times in my apartment despite the fact that Nevin had a key. Paul told me what had happened with Angela at the end of the summer of our affair. "She found out I was cheating a couple times," he said. "There were movie tickets I couldn't explain, a message you left. She learned the remote code on my answering machine."

It didn't surprise me that she'd found out. When I saw Paul, I had often been able to tell she'd been in his apartment; she must have had the same ability with me. It was as if he couldn't fully exorcise us after we'd been there, because he lacked that dollhouse sensibility of women, the attention to tiny detail that I was sure Angela and I shared.

"Did she break up with you?" I asked.

"She threatened to. I keep telling her I'll be faithful. She always takes me back. I never am," he confessed.

I found it odd that he'd turned out like me—chronically unfaithful—with his perfect family, his perfect set of choices. I wondered what it was in him that paralleled the force in me that, at the last minute, could not bear intimacy, had to breach it.

Another time, I finally told him that my mother had died, that she'd been dying all along.

"This has been going on the whole time I've known you?" he asked.

I nodded into his chest as he held me.

"I would like to see you happy," he commented. I supposed that, like my co-clerk Ben, he'd seen my sadness the whole time I had thought I'd concealed it.

I nodded again. I couldn't trust myself to speak.

"I'm so glad it's over," he said.

That was the dominant fact for him, I realized: no one was feeling that pain now, my mother no longer existed. I wanted a little for him to cry, to take from him the coin of his tears, but the wish was so unrealistic. Any emotion he could muster over my mother's death would feel forced to both of us, because he hadn't known about her dying while it was happening. It was simply history to him now—the kind of inconsequential ancient history that I'd once argued to him could just as well be fiction. His parents were alive; he'd been too young when his grandparents had died to be allowed to see it happen. He did not know his mortality by heart the way I did, I thought, didn't know with emotional certainty that this body that he slept with would someday die.

Still, I was happy to have told him, as if it were part of a long process of beginning to be honest. As if, even continuing my infidelities, I had a vague sense of the possibility of another, better life, lived another way.

Chapter Eight

————

BY THE FOLLOWING summer, when my clerkship was ending, I almost felt free of my mother's death. I'd had a year to
adjust, a year in which my life had been at least relatively calm
and steady. Nevin planned to be in Europe playing chess most
of the summer, so our relationship was on hold; we only spoke
on the phone. There seemed no reason that I could not work
quietly on the contract and corporate cases I'd been assigned
and let the imperceptible process of healing from my mother's
death work itself out in me in tiny ways, as the body heals itself when cut, until it was finished.

I learned about the risk almost randomly. Because I'd left
for college before my mother was diagnosed with Alzheimer's
disease, I'd never spoken with any of her doctors, and if my
aunt had known about the risk of my getting the disease, she
hadn't said anything, except for her single comment about my
having it on both sides of my family. But I had read some-

where that Alzheimer's disease was genetic and I wanted to know just how genetic it was. Very much so, it turned out, from what I was able to skim from an on-line service that included medical articles. I did the math: My mother had died of the disease in 1992, at the age of fifty-three. It had certainly begun disabling her—affecting her vision and her mind—by 1989, when I graduated from college and she was fifty. And my intuition was that it had begun at least several years earlier. I was twenty-five. If I had the gene, then my life was already, in effect, at least half over.

I felt as if I'd lived in darkness, gradually discerning outlines until my eyes became accustomed to the dark, the pupils growing large enough to take in everything there was to see— first, the meaning of this death; now, that I might die that way, too. I made a doctor's appointment to find out with greater certainty what my risk was. I couldn't really discern it from the jargon of the articles.

Waiting for my appointment, I read more and more about the disease, and something I read disturbed me: one of the ways Alzheimer's disease manifests itself, I learned, is by an intense and growing irritability that later becomes anger, directed even at close family members and friends. I knew that I could not remember exactly when the worst of my mother's angers began—whether they began in my childhood, or after the divorce, or even later. I thought about the diffuse, paranoid anger she'd directed at me in high school and realized that even then it could have been a symptom of the disease. I realized that although the anger my mother expressed must have derived in part from herself, in part it was like a storm that affected us both. I did not know how to judge her anymore. All my excuses for leaving were being taken from me.

The referral I received was to Dr. Cecil Gitell at a genetics center in the area. He turned out to be an elfin man with a white beard and a reassuring demeanor. Accustomed to giving genetic bad news, he had boxes of tissues in his office. He gave me all the time I needed, for which I was grateful.

He asked me what I did and I told him I was a law clerk. Then I explained why I'd come. I told him about my mother's disease and that she had died recently.

"I'm sorry," he said.

"It was for the best," I replied. "What she had was not . . . it was not a kind of life for anyone to have," I finished lamely.

"I know," he said. "It's a terrible thing."

"I read that I have a risk of getting it, too," I said.

"Was it an autopsy diagnosis?" he asked. "Other diseases can be confused with Alzheimer's."

"Yes," I told him.

He nodded. Then he took out a sheet of paper and asked me to tell him the cause of death of each of my relatives, as far back as I could remember. I told him about my grandparents' deaths—none had died of Alzheimer's disease, but one had died young. I told him I didn't know about my great-grandparents' deaths.

"Could you call a relative and find out?" he asked me.

"My family's estranged," I told him. "It would be very hard for me to do that."

"That's okay," he said. "We have enough information."

He put aside my scanty, useless family tree, full of blank spaces: anonymous ancestors, all the generations of people lost to me. (In the articles I have read on Alzheimer's research since then, I am amazed at the researchers' ability to trace genetic lines in so many destroyed families.) I thought of the family tree I had found in Sarah's notebook long ago: the shine of her crosshatched pencil marks on the darkened half of the page.

Dr. Gitell told me, carefully, that I was right: my mother's autopsy diagnosis meant that I had a genetic risk of getting her type of Alzheimer's disease, too. Unlike the more common gene for late-onset Alzheimer's disease, the gene for early-onset Alzheimer's, starting in the victim's forties or fifties, was strongly genetic, he said. It had a high chance of being passed down from generation to generation.

"What about my grandparents not having had it?" I asked. "Then it couldn't be a dominant gene, right?"

I had a grade-school knowledge of dominant and recessive genes, only enough to know that dominant genes always showed if you had them, but recessive genes didn't necessarily do so.

"That's not certain," he said. "It's possible that your grandparents died of other causes before it could show."

"There's also another possibility," he added. "Your mother could actually have been the first in the family to have it. Early-onset Alzheimer's can be a gene mutation, like dwarfism. The relevant gene could have spontaneously mutated while she was in the womb. So even though her parents didn't have the gene, she did—just as a dwarf can be born from full-size parents."

Then he told me a story of a dwarf who had corrected a misconception he'd had about dwarfism. I'm sure the story was meant to be amusing, that it *was* amusing, but I couldn't listen. All I remember is the image of the agitated dwarf stridently lecturing the geneticist while standing on his desk. I understood that I was now the counterpart of that dwarf: emotionally invested in this hard science, unable to step back from it.

"What are my chances of inheriting the gene?" I asked him. I had to press him before he'd tell me.

Finally he said, "Maybe 50 percent. It could be as high as that. It could be less. It's hard to know."

"Can I be tested for the gene?" I asked. I'd heard doctors could give genetic tests in families with a high incidence of breast cancer or Huntington's disease.

He said there might be a test, perhaps within five years or so.

"But," he added, "you should think for a while about whether you really want to know. Particularly now. You're in the bloom of life. You're what, in your twenties now?"

"Twenty-five."

"You don't need to think about all this for a long time. You shouldn't think that more information is always better. It's not always true."

"I might do something different with my life if I knew I had less time," I countered.

"Why don't you just do what you want now?" he asked.

"I don't know," I said. I did not have a good answer to his question, I realized.

"There's the issue of children," I pointed out. "And it would be fairer to someone I married if he could know. When am I supposed to tell someone this?" I asked plaintively, thinking aloud.

After I said this, I felt immediately embarrassed, as if the conversation were verging into therapy. In the shock of knowing my risk for the first time, I spoke to Dr. Gitell as I ordinarily would not have spoken to a doctor.

"Not on the first date," the doctor answered.

I smiled. Someone else might have found the remark insensitive, but it was tonic to me that he took this less seriously than I did. I needed someone to.

Then his voice was gentler. "I've talked to a lot of patients in similar situations, where the test would lead to a 'no hope' diagnosis. Many of them decided after reflection not to be tested. There isn't any cure or treatment for Alzheimer's, and we don't predict one. With a 'no hope' diagnosis, a lot of institutions won't test. They worry about suicide if people test positive, and the liability. Some will test you, though."

"I'm certain that I want to know," I told him.

"Okay," he said. "It would help if you could keep a sample of your mother's brain tissue, even given the autopsy diagnosis. It would still be useful to be able to compare her DNA against yours."

"I think I can do that," I said. I knew Betty had sent my mother's brain to be autopsied, then sent it to a research center at a university. I thought samples must have been kept.

"You should write us every year or so if you want to know about the possibility of a test," he said.

I walked out of the doctor's office shaky, wavering. I felt as if a dark corona surrounded me, as if I were at one remove from the living world. I was not supposed to be able to know, at the age of twenty-five, the likely means and time of my own death. My body, I thought, was supposed to be programmed —but only to grow, and only until adulthood. After that I was entitled to be free. Now I might have this freedom, or it might always have been illusory. The nursing home reports my aunt had sent me could be the chronicle of my own future, messages sent back to me through time, as warnings. My brain could break exactly as my mother's had, in the same predetermined way, like a glued-together cup breaking along old fault lines, bearing the map of its own shattering. Perhaps nothing separated me from my mother but age and time, when

I had thought we, our lives, were so profoundly different. Had I been her child after all, deeply hers, down to the genes, all these years?

For a few hours that day, I wandered around downtown Boston, as if only when I returned to my apartment would I really have to live the life—with its new, terrible risk—that I now knew was mine. I saw a movie downtown and I sat for a long time in a café. I was reluctant to return to my small apartment. For a moment, I found comfort in thinking of it as belonging to someone else, a different person who bore this risk while I did not: "Her books," I thought. "Her things. Her problems." I wanted to rid myself of my inalienable life, to disappear into another without a trace. But later I returned home, and drew on the mantle of my life again.

Sitting there, I looked at the two diplomas on my desk, still waiting to be framed, written in Latin, their pomp an attempt to remove them from everyday life: ordinariness, impeachability, loss. I felt contempt for their paper safety, ready to be punctured, punched through in a moment, or peeled back easily: a safety so revocable, so very thin.

I began to touch the edges of my teeth with the pads of my fingers, moving up to the soft gums under which it is possible to feel the skull beginning. I thought about how all the body's processes take place between the thin, pierceable veil of the skin and the bones' hard and basic core. I thought about my animal, perishable, asymmetrical heart. And the psychological place of rest that I had found, in adjusting to the fact of my mother's death, began slowly to crumble, becoming finally not a place but instead a process of disintegration.

I felt that the death I sensed so strongly in me should be easily visible, yet all I saw in the mirror when I looked was a scared woman, otherwise healthy. If my face showed my heart, I thought, it would be full of strike marks, scars torn to show, ruinous scars twisted past healing. But it was smooth as glass, the skin of my face, according to the mirror. If I was sick, why wasn't I sick *now?* It seemed to me so strange that I might be invisibly scheduled to die yet still be fine for such a long time. That I might bear somewhere an inscrutable mark, internal and deadly and hidden.

AFTER I LEARNED my risk, I began to be gripped by fear at odd, random times. The fear would come and go unpredictably; it was as if I would walk into a spiderweb and panic, intent on ridding myself of something I couldn't see. Sometimes I would sit at work paralyzed by fear that what I would write in a judicial opinion would be wrong, a misinterpretation of the law. Sometimes my anxiety verged on the physical, as if I were exhausted but needed to stay awake to finish something. Before I learned my risk, I had a strong fear of aging, seeing the features I most disliked exaggerate themselves—low breasts, a slight tendency to heaviness. Afterward, I realized it was normal aging that I wanted, for which I would give anything.

I decided to do the one practical thing I could to allay my fear, and I asked the forensic center in Tucson to Federal Express to me the slides of my mother's brain tissue. They agreed to do it. They said the rest of her brain was in the lab of a professor who studied Alzheimer's disease.

The slides came. They were perfect squares of glass bordered with thick white cardboard that slid around in a small plastic container. I took the slides out of the box gingerly, thinking of the paper-thin slices of brain tissue trapped within them. My hands shaking, I held them up to the light, but the slides were too dark to decipher with the naked eye, mercifully inscrutable except to a microscope. Like my own body, they held a hidden, frustrating message: the map of my mother's life. Maybe the map of my own as well. A particular destiny, a fate. The description of what might be my inheritance, her legacy. They would have to wait, in their box, to be read.

It made me feel better to be able to keep them there, as if I had the answer somewhere. Someday (someday soon, I hoped), I would take the canister of slides and pass it across a counter to someone, and my fate would then be, very literally, out of my hands. I keep the slides in a box in my apartment now, for the time when I decide to take the test. I am eager to give over my blood or a scraping of my skin for it.

NEVIN HAD NOT believed what I said about the genetic risk when I first told him about having read the article, shortly before I saw Dr. Gitell. He told me I couldn't possibly be right. And he did not have much to say to comfort me after my appointment. After he returned to Boston at the end of the summer, he left me, and it hurt me more than any earlier breakup—even though I had cheated on him with Paul, even though he had never been able to comfort me. I think it was because he'd said he loved me so many times before I learned the risk, and then he'd stopped saying it as often, it seemed, afterward; and then, of course, he had stopped saying it at all.

I wonder still how I can ask someone else to take this on. It has taken me so long to be able to live with this risk. And I will never be able wholly to ignore it. From what I have read, the fifty-fifty estimate that Dr. Gitell tentatively gave, as a maximum, still seems about right. If the chance were less, then perhaps the risk would not affect me as much. Then I could think: The odds are that I won't get it. It is the split into two equally possible lives that I cannot ignore.

One part of me feels sure that, for abandoning my mother, I will be sentenced to live out her death: a perfect punishment, more fitting than a person could design, more exact than any the law metes out, embedded in the body and inescapable. But I know in my heart that genes are not a true punishment —because nothing my mother did could ever, ever have merited the punishment she received, the slow dementia she was destined to suffer.

Another part of me hopes regardless of the basis and believes that the negative result will come. Often I remind myself sensibly that all I feel, and have felt, because of my genetic risk may be for nothing. All my tears may be as vapor; all my dodges, evasions of a phantom. This is only a risk, after all, not a reality in the blood. It is a kind of vanity to feel this when other people are really dying, dying now. Remember, I caution myself, you are not necessarily dying.

It would be difficult for me to ask someone I love to go through this long process, this alternation of hope and fatalism, to join me in this nowhere place, awaiting the test result, exiled from time—or to understand why anyone would want to say yes to such a request. I am still haunted by the question I asked Dr. Gitell: the question of when to tell. He was right, of course: not on the first date. But soon after, I think. More honest than I once was, I know now that secrecy is unfair, damaging. And after telling, why go on? I don't really believe people fall in love that fast, so fast they cannot help themselves from falling off this cliff with me. And, anyway, why would I want to tempt anyone to make the Faustian bargain of loving me—only, perhaps, to have this abyss of sadness in the end? I am left with a paradox: I would like to be with someone who would want to stay with me despite a positive test result, who loved me unconditionally, yet I know that if I did test positive, I would feel compelled to leave anyone I was seeing, because the positive result seems too much to allow someone else to take on.

One man I dated later, Adrian, did accept my risk. He told

me: "I would want to marry you before you knew." He said he'd loved me passionately ever since we'd met in college. And I thought he knew what it was he was accepting. His aunt and uncle had two children who had already been diagnosed as terminally ill, with a degenerative genetic disease; he was familiar with their day-by-day struggle.

Adrian and I are equally romantic: if I were in his situation, in love with someone with a genetic risk like mine, I think I would say just what he did. There could have been a happy ending—he is brilliant and kind, handsome and successful. Yet I promptly cheated on Adrian, with someone who couldn't possibly stay with me—a man who knew he would marry someone Jewish, who was good to me but made no pretense of loving me, and whom I knew in my heart, even at the time, that I liked but would not love. I felt as if I couldn't help myself.

I told Adrian that I had cheated on him and he was smart enough to leave me. Afterward, I was disgusted with myself, as well I should have been. Why couldn't I accept this love? I had proven to myself for so long that I could live without being loved by another person. Now it was as if I had to continue to prove this to everyone else, compulsively, forever. It seemed to show that there was no solution for me. If I didn't tell a lover about my history, I'd feel no intimacy, and then I'd cheat. But what I discovered with Adrian was that when I *did* tell someone, I'd cheat out of fear—fear of realness, of romance, and, overwhelmingly, the fear of giving someone, in the end, only the awful gift of my death. Viewed in the most charitable light, my cheating on Adrian may have been the only way to stop us from marrying. A last resort.

I still do imagine getting married sometimes, though I can hardly peg my life on it. Sometimes I think there is a kind of backwards valor to being forced to define my life as about not marriage, but work. At least, I think, I will not be one of those women who foregoes a career for marriage and children—the way my mother did.

When I am weaker, though, I imagine a wedding. It would happen at night with the bridesmaids wearing black velvet, under cover of dark as if in secrecy, as if in time of war, taking advantage of the darkness and yet with candles lit against it. I envision its banquet laid out as a dark feast, with heavy wines and a licorice-based cake, the table laden with dark flowers, purple or blue.

I think I imagine it this way because there is no lightness to a wedding in the consciousness of this sorrow, this risk. But there might be love.

Afterward, I imagine being faithful, and content. I imagine that there would be a certainty in my heart at last—whether or not I could know the truth about my death.

AT THE TIME I learned about my risk, I'd never really thought carefully about whether, or how much, I wanted a child—I was only twenty-five at the time. An ex-boyfriend once said to me (at someone else's wedding) that he thought I would make a great wife but he couldn't see me as a mother. I agreed then that I was not the "mother type"—secretly thinking that maybe my own mother had not given me a way to be one. I began to disqualify myself, in my mind, from having children. Older now, I know I want at least the choice to have a child, perhaps in part because it now is barred to me. I am nearing the age my mother was when she gave birth to me, thirty. And I feel crazily as if fate could make me pregnant immaculately then—as it may immaculately make me die at a later age, the last she reached.

I think often about the child I might have. I imagine a small girl: lulled by an automatic rocker; crowing atop a playground slide, waiting on the flat bench before deciding to slide down; or shimmying, shoulders moving, through tunnels on her curved stomach. Yet even as I envision her, I feel her disappearing, like an Edward Gorey child rendered in black and white, line-drawn, straw-haired, a bit sickly: a small consumptive who fades away.

She disappears for me if the result of the test is positive. One of the responsibilities of having a child, to me, is that you do your best not to die before she can grow up. And she disappears, I think, even if I cannot be tested. This disease strikes after people usually have children, so evolution cannot select for it. The trait could descend down through generations, the genetic code immortal even as its bearers die—creating a doomed family line like a cameo bracelet of successive heads. The cruelty of this mutation, created in a moment, could persist forever: children watching their parents die too soon and then growing up themselves only to show their children early death. It could reach over generations, in perpetuity further than even a will legally could. It will stop only if someone chooses to stop it. I want to be the one who chooses that. It will make me feel free to say: This genetic curse stops with me. My death is the last it will take. There is an end to suffering, in the world.

It is not that I worry a child would resent my choice to give her life. It is that I worry she could love life too much to bear knowing (or fearing) all her life when and how she will lose it. But then I also think of people like the writer Jorge Luis Borges, knowing he would go blind because of a congenital illness, and of his parents, knowing—yet deciding to have this child, deciding that a blind life was still worth living. There is no perfect life, I know that. And I might have a brave, impetuous child who would not worry and would be devoted to living, in love with it—who would not live in fear. Is it a loss if, with all the people who will be born, my child will not be among them? I'm not sure. She will be unloved and unloving. But she will also be untroubled, unhaunted, and exempt from pain. And she will not die.

That child: to imagine her is a suspension of disbelief, as love is. I have a space in myself for her already cleared. I may die with it empty. My test result will be her real conception, if she is to be born.

Chapter Nine

———

WHEN I LATER accepted another clerkship, with a New York City trial judge, it did not escape me that, in addition to being a brilliant judge, she seemed the perfect mother to her son, or that she was the age my mother had been when she died. Her courthouse was in Manhattan's Foley Square, towering over Chinatown's painted signs in red and yellow and the green of jade. I moved to Chelsea and started a life there.

This clerkship had people in it—witnesses, attorneys, sometimes defendants, and often jurors. I was thankful for this. Having the people who were involved in the cases there in court was, in a way, only a small change from my previous appellate clerkship—my work was still legal—but it meant a great deal to me. This small change in my job seemed to correspond to a change in my life as a result of which I began to be closer to human, less a creature of my mind. I began to realize that I wanted to be more than a very good, technically proficient lawyer—an infinitely patient legal spider building an analytical web, glistening strand by glistening strand. I wanted to care more about other people's fates, to be less preoccupied with my own selfish sorrow. This was a small step that way, I thought.

Now I could see the criminal defendants whose cases were before the judge, when they appeared in court to plead guilty or to be tried or sentenced. I often thought about what would happen to them in prison, how the years of wasted time would grow in them like a patch of numbness spreading around an anesthetic needle. One defendant was a low-level "mule" who'd carried drugs and likely known little about the conspiracy in which he'd been involved. Another was a desperate businessman who'd lost his parents' retirement money, then tried to make it back by fraud. Another was a "bank robber"—a teller who'd walked out with a sack of cash one day and found the FBI at his apartment that night. What they had done was wrong, certainly, but it seemed to me so human to be fallible in these ways, for a person in desperate circumstances to accept a chance to make money quickly, by an act that did not require violence. But the judge could not help them; there was no forgiveness for them in the law.

I identified with the defendants a bit, probably in a very romanticized way given the guns some of them must have carried and all that they were willing to do. I often watched a defendant as he pled guilty and looked for what was there in his eyes, what human quality—whether resignation or resentment or fear. Like the defendants, I dreaded that the punishment to come would be harsher than I could bear.

I began then to know that I wanted to become a criminal defense lawyer, to try to convince judges and juries that defendants are as real as themselves: as innocent, as guilty. And to demonstrate to myself that there are people in life, some of them lawyers, who will defend you in your lowest hour, who will not turn away.

PAUL HAD MADE the opposite decision, it turned out, becoming a prosecutor with the Manhattan DA's office. He prosecuted violent crime: murder and assault. He put people away. I knew this from friends. I knew from them, too, that he'd gotten engaged to Angela at the start of the summer, a few months ago. But he called me nonetheless, soon after I started work.

"I broke off my engagement," he said. "Can I see you?"

I said yes in an instant. I'd thought that, because of the engagement, I'd never see him again in my life; Angela would forbid it.

The first time Paul and I saw each other, near my Chelsea apartment, we air-kissed awkwardly, bumping into each other at first, then trying again. He carried a leather satchel fat with documents. I knew they might be indictments or arguments in favor of imprisonment and, for the first time, the power he had seemed real to me.

Paul's job had given him a bit of a clean-cut, Eliot Ness look. Mine had made me try to appear more grown-up, because I dealt with attorneys so often. We both seemed to me neater, older, with more serious faces and shorter hair; broken a little by the world, maybe, and making concessions to it. We agreed that we both liked being "in the trenches," there with the trials. I was still attracted to him: to the aggression he brought to his job, to his pure certainty that he was in the right. I wondered what it meant, that I'd chosen for myself someone who was such a natural prosecutor. I thought that he would seduce juries as he'd seduced me—like me they would go with him, do what he wanted them to do. They would find him arrogant but charming, as I had. I imagined for a moment that a jury verdict for the government would put him in ecstasy, his eyes half closed for just a second to savor it. It would be pure pleasure, as from sex or sports: the girl conquered, the ball swishing through the hoop, the moment of freedom just after conquest when you know that whatever it is that you want to strike home, will.

He told me about his job: about cooperators so eager to implicate defendants that they weren't credible on the witness stand; crack-addict witnesses who would not show up for trial; the difficult ethical decision of whom among a group of co-conspirators to "flip" so that he or she would testify for the government. Betrayal was his bread and butter, it turned out: co-defendants turning state's evidence, agreeing to testify.

"Tell me about the engagement," I said.

"There's not that much to tell," he said. "She gave me the marriage ultimatum and I couldn't decide. Finally I did propose, but she started complaining. I didn't get her a ring for a couple of weeks, I didn't want her to move in with me immediately, and so on. Then she told me we couldn't live in my apartment after we got married; we'd have to find a new one, which I would pay for. I felt like I was just taking over from her father the job of supporting her."

"How did you break it off?" I asked.

"I got drunk with Emmet"—his best friend from college— "and I told her. I don't know that I could go through it again."

"Do you still think about getting married?" I asked.

"I dodged that bullet," he said and laughed. Someone else would have found him crass, but his remark reminded me of my favorite thing about him: that he was free. He could walk away from anything; he could choose anything. And there was some confidence in him, not entirely foolish, that would make him believe his choices were correct.

Even though Paul was single, we did not sleep together. He still wanted to; I wanted to but could not. This was a small choice, unremarkable to anyone else. To me, it was as if a spell had been broken. I thought there was some partial love between us; he said as much, and so did I. Of course, he loved me only if his love was irresponsible. Yet this small love was real; I still think it was. But the lesson had been ground into me too hard, over too many years, that loving him—or the idea, or memory, of him—would not save me.

Chapter Ten

———

I FANTASIZE ABOUT knowing. I envision opening the envelope that contains the test result. I would like to do it in private. I hope that I will not be required to do it in a doctor's office or with a "genetic counselor" watching me anxiously, waiting to give me counsel that I don't want. It is a private thing: I would far prefer that it be simply me and the envelope. The message is mine—a message of my fate, my destiny. The secret design of my life: it makes me think of the ancient idea of the homunculus in the sperm. As if the woman I will become has been there in me in miniature all the time.

Here is how I imagine it: *In front of me on the table is the sealed report, in its thin white envelope marked* CONFIDENTIAL *by the genetics center. One part of the wide V-shaped closure has become unstuck. It is beginning to unseal itself. In the past, I have been confident about test results—my anticipation more than half sweet, not really fearful, the en-*

velopes quickly ripped open to reveal my grades in college and law school, the bar exam result. All those human grades: appealable, revisable, related to what I'd written, the product of the hard work of weeks. I opened those other envelopes almost avariciously. I don't know if I can bring myself to open this one at all.

I stare at the envelope. I run my fingers along its edges and play with its half-broken seal. Then I put it down. The person who sent this, I realize, must have envisioned this moment, too. It was an act with some moral weight and consequence simply to place this envelope in the mail. I cannot help believing the result will be positive. But I remind myself that it is a rebellion even to open this. If the envelope contains a death sentence, it is one that was penned before I was born, one that I was never intended to read. To read this now is to thwart some hidden plan, to break the security of my body and learn the confidential information of its most interior chambers. To learn its agenda for me.

I reach for the envelope and tear it open. The paper curls away from the ripped edge. I easily slide out the thin report, which is neatly folded into thirds. I unfold it. What is written so many times into my body I read now in this report signed by a mortal hand in a human script: that I have tested positive and will die. Mine will be the second death from this gene, just like the first, just like my mother's.

This is the "no hope" diagnosis that Dr. Gitell described,

but there is a way I find hope in it. The fear I had of this has ended at last, and with it the waiting. At the same time that it devastates me, this piece of paper resolves me. It makes me real. At least this single sheet of paper no longer holds me in its liege; I am not its creature. Instead, I am a free person, with twenty years to spend as flesh, profligately or cautiously as I choose.

That is the hopeful way in which I envision learning my diagnosis. I don't know why exactly—maybe it is a crazy, or a transitory, thing—but when I imagine this moment, I imagine feeling as if I've been given a gift, not as if something has been stolen from me. But I may be wrong. I may be destroyed by it, this "no hope" diagnosis, if it comes. It may destroy me even as it makes me know who I am. I would still prefer that —prefer to be that destroyed person—over not knowing.

I fantasize about another moment, too—as if it will protect me to go to the end of my imagination and face what I find there. It is the moment of my suicide, if a positive result should come. My mother did not know what was happening when the disease came to her and as a consequence she did not have the chance to take her own life. But I will know, as soon as I can be tested, long before the illness comes—and I will have the choice to stop it. I will not be impotent again, as I was with my mother, watching disaster come, powerless to prevent it. Nor will I be wheeled around in a nursing home, becoming a stream of money that demands that nurses minister to a body from which the mind is absent. I may live without history as long as I can, writing myself notes about what has happened that morning or on the previous day. But one thing is certain: I will watch for my own unraveling. My handwriting will never spread to scrawl, my words never slur to murmur. For what it is worth, it will be different for me. If the time comes, I will take death and not wait for it—even if, until then, I always will fear the possibility of this death and resent it, and rail against it in my heart and ask why.

I believe that there is a right to die. To me, if there is any right that is inalienable or natural, it is this one: the basic right of each person in the body, and its breath, and its heartbeat, and its thought, and in the end of all these. I feel that the right inheres in me as deeply as does the risk, as deeply as my death itself may. It saddens me that, as the law now stands, if I test positive, I may someday have to take my life surreptitiously, that it may be illegal for me officially to be helped by anyone in this, the hardest act of my life. Still, at least I will have warning; at least I will be able to choose.

I have thought of using a gun, but, knowing little about it, I imagine there would have to be time spent learning to shoot at cardboard figures in "self-defense." This would be ironic, of course, because it would really be myself that I would envision shooting, and the idea would be not to defend myself but to die. There is no training for that: it is reinvented each time, by each person who chooses it.

Take an old straight razor instead, still flecked with tiny dark hairs from shaving, still with these traces of life; not as sharp as it might be. I clean the razor before beginning. Then I fit my fingers around each of my supinated wrists in turn. I see the crease in the skin from all the times they've been bent since I was born, and the light blue veins, the blood contained under the skin. I cut first one wrist, wincing, and then the other. Vertically: I have read that you are supposed to do it vertically, not across.

I lie still, and my mind is a cup for all my life's memories, which rest inside it intact. I can have access to any of these, call them forth: it is an embarrassment of memory. My mother's mind was its own ghost at the end. Mine remains the sum of everything I have known that has imprinted itself on me, cut its paths in my mind. I am glad I have chosen to die this way, with the sudden end of memory, the absolute dark, and not with the twilight of a gradual forgetting.

After a moment, my body, startled, rouses itself to fill the cuts with blood. The blood flows profusely, profligately, as if there were a liquid rising in my heart to displace it. Freeing blood frees emotion in me, a sign of my heart's life even as it is the way I die. I lie back light-headed and the stains spread evenly around my upturned wrists, like two red flowers opening into their full promise.

STILL, THE DEATHS one imagines are only that.

It occurs to me that if I truly loved my mother, and had

great courage, I might see a positive test result as a strange (even an insane) privilege—the privilege of wholly knowing my mother, a recapitulation of her pain after I balked so long from even imagining it. The privilege of not being as others are: saved by the division of bodies, by birth itself.

If I died the way she did, waited out the long process, I would know her anger, her depression, her despair. I might perhaps understand her at last. I would see the door she went through, walk down that long corridor with her, my lost mother. I would be close to blind with her in the same sad chaos, feel the foundations weaken, the floor give way. I would leave with her the house of order, the house of law, the house of housekeeping: of rationality itself. I would walk out with her into the house of chaos, like a child being led by the hand.

Someone stronger than I am could see love in that. I see only terror. At best, I see it as a proper comeuppance for the arrogance of thinking I could leave, or as partial expiation for my leaving, since I may have to suffer all she suffered for myself. Finally, I am not her, my mother; and I would do anything not to become her; and if empathy is one escape from the terror of my strange condition of risk, then I do not choose it. I choose to balk. I choose, as I have always chosen, to abandon her. And I would choose this forever, again and again, in hell if necessary. It has come to define who I am: the daughter who left her mother—the bad daughter, the one who did not stay. The love in me for her did not die out, not entirely. But the leaving in me was so much stronger. It was ruthless to have me, it made me ruthless, and I belonged to it in the end.

This is a taboo story, I know, for it's the stories of reconciliation that are told over and over—the birth mother reunited with her child given up for adoption, the long-lost found, the feud ended—and not the stories of leaving. I always think that if people really knew me—I mean, knew me at the deepest level—they wouldn't like me. As if I'm harder than they are. A worse person. But would other people really have chosen to care for a mother who wasn't loving, who was often angry, who was often simply gone? Would they have resisted the freedom that school could bring, the perfectly timed luck of the escape it offered? Should I fear that they would have? Feel better if I think that, like me, they would not have? I do not know the inner hearts of the people around me; maybe they do not either—mostly, people are not tested like this.

All that divides me from the many who have not known this, or been this, is the privilege of their not having to know it, or be it. Yet I have to concede that this privilege is, in its way, a superiority. I have to bow, at least, to that good fortune. Even if what they have is simply luck and not a quality of character, there is a quality of character that their luck leaves intact and that now, in me, is devastated. I know the quality; some days I can simulate it. And always, I feel the space where it should be.

I WISH SOMETIMES that my mother could talk to me, her cold, solitary daughter. I wish I could hear her voice—whether drunken or sober, whether slurred or articulate, I don't care. It could be a ragged, intensely corporeal voice, like the bellow of the retarded or the deaf. Or a voice spoken from a raw and reddened throat, as painful to speak as it is to hear. But I imagine it finally as a quiet voice—the voice that perhaps spoke in her, unheard, within that frozen body I visited in Tucson.

I do imagine her voice sometimes, telling me I am forgiven. But it never seems really to be her. It makes me wonder if the dead, in their imagined visitations, ever do speak, or if what speaks in us is the sheared-off part of the self that belongs to them. Be less abstract, I admonish myself—I mean, the part of me that belongs to her.

Betty once said to me over the phone that my mother and father were happy together when they lived in Hoboken, New Jersey, and my father was finishing graduate school. She said they lived near a coffee factory and would find grounds on their windowsills; their apartment always smelled nicely of it. My father received his doctorate the day I was born and accepted a job offer in Hawaii. My mother thought it would be paradise, that they'd live in grass huts. She did not pack her vacuum cleaner. She took me, one year old, on the airplane, and when they got there she would go with me to the beach in the evenings, in an orange turtleneck if it was windy, and let me run there on the sand. She trusted my father enough to move alone with him, to let him be the only one she knew, to let her family life be the only one she had.

Sometimes I think of my mother then, at thirty, just a little older than I am now, of the leap of faith she made and how she was not strong enough for it, of how her body betrayed her so young, how she bore a mark within her that I may bear, too. And I believe that her faith in life should have been rewarded, not predestined to fail. I believe in a time before her angers began. I think of her as innocent, and later stricken, and I believe the disease was the root of it all. And I almost remember then, if I let myself, what it was to love her—long ago.

Acknowledgments

I COULD NOT have completed this book without the help and support of Melanie Thernstrom, and I owe her a great debt both as a friend and as a writer. I would also like to thank my agent, Henry Dunow, and my editor, Elisabeth Scharlatt, for her skill and kindness and the care she took with the manuscript.

It was Alex Johnson who first told me that I could become a writer, and I am very lucky to have had her and Mary Robison as teachers. The Cornell M.F.A. program provided me with the crucial time and financial support that I needed to write this book. My teachers there provided invaluable help —especially Alison Lurie, Dan McCall, Stephanie Vaughn, and Carey Harrison.

Many friends also provided important suggestions— especially Morgan Belford, Jason Brown, Mike Chen, William

Chettle, Sherry Colb, Junot Diaz, Michael Dorf, Jennifer Dworkin, James Forman, Jr., Erez Kalir, Jonathan Levitsky, Joanne Mariner, Joshua Paschman, Nina Revoyr, and David Vann.